Yes...Minister?

Patterns of Christian Service

❖❖❖❖❖❖❖❖❖❖❖❖❖❖❖❖❖❖❖❖❖❖❖❖❖❖❖❖❖❖

JIM COTTER

SHEFFIELD
CAIRNS PUBLICATIONS
1992

ISBN 1 870652 15 0

First published 1992

Further copies of this book are obtainable from
Cairns Publications
47 Firth Park Avenue, Sheffield s5 6HF

Printed by J. W. Northend Ltd
Clyde Road, Sheffield s8 0TZ

£1.00

CONTENTS

In celebration
of
the fiftieth anniversaries
of
a birth and a baptism
23 August and 15 November 1942

and dedicated
to all those whose call to ministry
has in the past or to this day
been unrecognized and unfulfilled
by reason of gender or sexual preference

PREFACE

THIS book is written in celebration of a particular anniversary of one person's birth and baptism – his first golden jubilee, a year after the seven sevens, one to be marked in a special way. It is by circumstance of timing also the silver jubilee of his entering public ministry in the Church.

I approach the celebration of the first anniversary with joy and delight, amazed at nearing the age of fifty. But I find I want to be no more than quietly thankful for the other, though there are many in such circumstances who would wish to mark it by an occasion of splendour and partying, with a Eucharist of particular gratitude. I am reluctant to do that, not because I at all regret the last twenty-five years, but because it would seem to exaggerate the significance of one kind of ministering, giving it a status beyond its worth. I am also reluctant because I am aware that so many of my contemporaries are not able to fulfil the potential they have for leadership in the Church because their sexuality is unusual or their gender unacceptable.

For reasons which are partly self-chosen and partly imposed upon me, and which have to do with sexuality, I have not taken as full a part in the ministry of leadership as I might otherwise have done. This has led me to reflect long and sometimes painfully on the different patterns of service that Christian people may be called to fulfil. And I have come to a number of convictions in the process.

First, I do not believe that anybody should be excluded from consideration for public ministry simply because of their sexual preference or gender. Second, I believe that the flourishing of churches depends upon leadership of an unusually dedicated kind, but one which needs – far more than is currently the practice – the values of service and sacrifice. Third, I believe that 'ordination' needs debunking, that we need perceptive children to shout that the emperors have no clothes, that all links with status and wealth should be broken, that the way of life should put off those who seek power. Fourth, I believe that our

humanity is most richly to be discovered in following Jesus
Christ, that Baptism declares this, the Eucharist celebrates it,
and day-to-day living is the place where it is embraced most
significantly. Thus humanity is more significant than the
Church, and Baptism more significant than any public ministry
with its beginning moments of 'ordination' or 'licensing'.

When we have learned how to celebrate the anniversaries of
our Baptism, then we may be in a position to know how
genuinely to celebrate the anniversaries of those in public office.
Not that I know how to go about celebrating the fiftieth anniversary of my Baptism in November. I am told I was baptised in
a Methodist Church on what was then called Temperance
Sunday, and after a sermon reminding the congregation of the
evils of alcohol, I was baptized – and hiccoughed throughout! So
I suppose I should be able to think of something which would
combine seriousness with light-heartedness. But I can't. It seems
that any such occasion would put oneself in the centre of the
picture – and too self-consciously so.

So I shall settle for a birthday dinner party among friends.
And I shall recollect that we are loved and called from before our
birth, that our birth is something we share with all humanity,
along with our death, and that it is right to invite those we love
and who have done much for us to celebrate an anniversary with
us. Christianity is about becoming fully human and abundantly
alive and there will be a quiet moment or two of gratitude that
Baptism started me along the particular human way of following
Christ and that the new relationship to the Christian community
recognized in 'ordination' has provided challenges to become a
more mature human being, challenges that have sometimes
been stumbling blocks, unlooked for but inevitable because of
our individual and corporate distortions. At other times there
have been challenges that have been relished, not least to write
and speak out, and to be alongside others in their training for
ministry.

It was that last challenge that provided the original impulse for
this book. Men and women training together on the Ministerial
Training Scheme in the Anglican Diocese of St Albans faced
many a confusion and contradiction as they reflected upon
their future. So I took some time to try and map those confusions

and discern possible directions. The result was distributed in duplicated form in the dying days of that particular technology! A few years on, with the issues of women's ministry coming to a moment of great decision in the Church of England, I felt moved to dust the original handbook and see what could be done with it. The result is the extended revision that is this book. But I do want to thank my students and colleagues in Hertfordshire and Bedfordshire for their companionship and stimulus during those years we worked together. And of course they may very well disagree with much of what is written here. We do not live in a settled time of clear agreements. But I hope a modest contribution of describing some of the patterns of Christian service may help to lessen the pain of confusion and release energy for a more fulfilling exercise of that service.

JIM COTTER
Sheffield, April 1992

Locating Ministries
in Society

The People of God:
Living the Love of God

How can the corporate life of the People
of God be so shaped as to reflect and
not deny what you most deeply believe to
be true about God? And what is – or might
be – your contribution to that life?

Begin the exploration of that question with 'Love'.
Remember that the end of that exploring
may well be to arrive where you started out
and to see that place as it really is – [1]
but you will not know what that means
until you have done the exploring.
'Love' may be central to Christianity,
but it may be easier to recognize in people
than to define in words,
above all to see it in the flesh and blood of Jesus,
revealing in word and deed the very heart of God.
Is your attention, your questioning, your living
focused on God – the God who really is *Love?*
Utter, joyous, pain-transforming Love?
Consistent and persistent, whatever the cost?
Do you *believe* that God accepts the *burden* of Love,
embracing all that causes harm,
never letting go,
never ultimately excluding, banishing, or destroying
that which is being created?

Pause and ask how you might for yourself express your belief that
God is Love...

Change the angle of the light a little:

> To free the world from enslavement to sin and death,
> Jesus, embodying the Love of God,
> absorbed evil without adding to it
> by acts of revenge and destruction,
> trusted that the power of Love can never be defeated,
> and gifted his followers
> with the same Spirit of unbreakable Love.

This is the invitation:

> Be in love with life,
> wrestle with the chaos and the pain,
> with your self and with others,
> spirit echoing Spirit,
> trusting in the victory of the vulnerable,
> glimpsing the peace, the wholeness,
> the spaciousness, the justice, and the joy
> that comes from following the Pioneer
> made perfect in suffering,
> striving and yearning and crying out
> from the depths and heights
> of the world's anguish and the world's bliss,
> and so becoming friends and partners of God
> in the divine creating...

You are called to follow One who shouldered a great heaviness
that it might be transmuted into the weight of glory. You must
therefore give no room to ambition for worldly success and the
exercise of power for its own sake. You are to be one of the
burden bearers of creation.[2]

So the first question again presses, in another form:

> If these things are true, how do the People of
> God, in particular their leaders, exercise their
> calling so as not to betray the God they serve?

Press the question home to that point within you that seeks a 'place' in the world, a 'status'. For if you are *already* accepted by God, created by God, delighted in by God, loved by God *for ever, whatever,* without conditions, whatever your twistedness out of true and however deep your wounds, and if you *accept* and receive that truth, if you say Yes to this God, then you live in the *givenness* of the only *status* that matters – friend, partner, lover of God.

> 'Conversion', whether by a flood of light or by
> dimmer shafts now and then, brings home the truth.

> 'Baptism' proclaims it and brings us into the
> company of those who also believe this truth.

> 'Discipleship' involves living out, with deepening
> commitment, a Yes to these questions:

>> Are you willing to reflect the Love of God in
>> your love of neighbour?

>> To Christ's invitation, 'Follow me,' are you
>> wholehearted in your response?

[What a simple invitation! But are you willing for that following to be permanent, to allow your relationship with the One who calls to be so alive that your mind and heart are constantly being formed, re-formed, and transformed?]

If you are being drawn towards some publicly recognized ministry, whether of leadership or of some other specific kind, you need to refer again and again to this heart of the Gospel and its challenge. The questions are starkly put at Baptism:[3]

> Do you turn to Christ?
> Do you repent of your sins?
> Do you renounce evil?

In more meditative form they might look like this:

> Are you willing to turn again to Christ,
> to turn to the deep things of God,
> to the Spirit of God moving within and among us,
> to God the Source and Goal of all that is,
> to the Mysterious Companion who is the Other
>   within us,
> to Christ, truly divine and truly human,
> living the way of unconditional love?

> Are you willing to turn your heart and mind
> daily in 'metanoia'[4] towards the God of Love,
> confessing your failures to love,
> forgiving yourself and others,
> and allowing yourself to be forgiven,
> absorbing hurts and not passing them on in a
>   spirit of retaliation?

> Are you willing to refuse the way of evil,
> of self-hatred and the hatred of others,
> to keep steadfastly to the true path,
> the Way, the Truth, and the Life of Jesus,
> to refuse the easy and comfortable way of unawareness
>   of all that is pressing upon us,
> rather to embrace and participate in the way of
>   compassion?

If Paul had Jesus in mind when he composed his hymn to Love when writing to the Corinthians, we are given an apt portrait of the follower of Jesus too:

> Love is patient and kind and knows no envy. Love never clings, is never boastful, conceited, or rude. Love is never selfish, never insists on its own way. Love is not quick to take offence. Love keeps no score of wrongs, nor gloats over the sins of others. Love rejoices in the truth. Love is tough: there is nothing it cannot face. Love never loses trust in human beings or in God. Love never loses hope, never loses heart. Love still stands when all else has fallen.[5]

How might such a portrait be translated from individual to community life? The People of God as a Community of the Love of God might show certain characteristics in its common life. They are cast here in the form of 'ten invitations':

> Be loyal to what you most deeply believe to be the will and way of the One who draws you by the still small voice, the voice which is often crowded out and which you find hardest to hear.

> Pay close attention simply to what is, asking the questions that arise from such contemplation, and seek to respond in truth – and so learn how to pray.

> Be thankful for small deeds of kindness as well as for greater blessings, and allow the spirit of gratitude to begin to embrace even the depths of seemingly intractable pain.

> Face illusion and betrayal with truth and courage, and be willing to delve ever deeper the mines of trust, forgiveness, and compassion.

> Live simply and sacrificially wherever greed and addiction rule, being aware of the need to reverence the earth and replenish what you have taken.

Work out and fulfil your contribution to the common good of society (and increasingly of the one world) of which you are citizens.

Welcome both neighbour and stranger as human beings to be accepted and valued in the same way as you would wish to be received.

Respond to the lonely with care and tact. Cast out fear by the presence and gentle persistence of prayerful and thoughtful affection. Share the pain of those whose stories reveal harm and shame, and be with them without intrusion or possession.

Refuse to act on prejudice or feelings of superiority where colour, class, religion, gender, or sexual preference are concerned; shun easy slogans and bear the discomfort of what is unresolved; listen silently to those who are different from yourself, whom you fear and mistrust, and do so without anxiety or hurry, and so avoid the strident claims of the self-righteous. Expect the Spirit of God to be alive and active – far beyond your own tribal boundaries.

Be expectant of the future while suspending your own expectations, trusting that it will bring gifts and graces beyond what you could predict or imagine, and so live in faith and hope.

Follow a narrow way.
Enter life through a needle's eye.
Accept constriction and limitation.
Exercise restraint over your own claims and desires.
Give up your defensive postures.
Lay down your life.

So you will discover, by living it, the way of sacrifice, of priestliness. Such are the marks of the royal priesthood of the People of God. Its secret is compassion.

Now the word 'priest' has had a troubled history. While it appropriately draws attention to the inner dynamic of the life of any leader of a Christian community, it is less appropriate as a title. Traditionally it refers to a level of being which is crucial to the one who is given that name. But does that apply only to 'priests' or to the whole royal priesthood? The word is never used as a title for an office bearer in the New Testament. There 'priest' and 'priesthood' refer either to Jesus himself or to the whole community of believers, which *participates* in the priesthood of Jesus.

> "...be yourselves built into a spiritual house, to be a holy priesthood, to offer in worship and life spiritual sacrifices to God through Jesus Christ... you are a royal priesthood... that you may declare the wonderful deeds of God."[6]

The writer of the Letter to the Hebrews understands God to be addressing Jesus thus:

"You are a priest for ever, after the order of Melchizedek."[7]

To appreciate the way in which the People of God share in that priesthood of Jesus, we do well to recall that Melchizedek, though a mysterious ancient figure about whom nothing is known, stands for a priesthood which (a) depends on God's initiative alone and not on family descent, and (b) is for ever, is eternal, without beginning or end, and not for this life only.

"Love is not self-contained, but self-expending and perfected in self-expenditure. The devotion of love in the sphere of Heaven is perfection of joy. But devotion of love to another in conditions of earth – even whilst it touches the highest possibilities of joy – means always more or less of pain. Devotion of self, in a world of sin and suffering, to the spiritual welfare of those who are enmeshed in suffering and sin, is forthwith, in external aspect, sacrifice; and, in inner essence, love. There is no essential contrast between sacrifice and love. Love, under certain disabling conditons, becomes sacrifice; and sacrifice is not sacrifice, except it be love."[8]

So we might reach this statement. The People of God are called to live the way of self-sacrificial Love, for ever, fulfilling God's Love as priestly men and women belonging to a new community. Priesthood is not a status or prerogative reserved to a few, with exclusive powers to match, but the *character* of the whole company of believers. Moreover, it is our *human* birthright. Becoming priestly is what makes us human. To be a Christian human being is to believe that the way of Jesus is the most complete way of growing to the full stature of our humanity, along with other human beings, co-creators with God and trustees of the rest of creation.

If you find yourself excluded from public ministry for reasons you do not regard as valid and yet are seeking to live your life by following Christ, you are bound to find it painful to remain a member of the Church. But it is still *your* Church as well as everybody else's, for the Church is that part of humanity which has already recognized, however partially, its centre in Christ. To leave the Church would be to leave humanity. You would be committing a kind of 'spiritual suicide'.[9] It may *feel* impossible at times to bear the tensions involved. But in whatever form it is laid upon you, the *necessity* of being priestly will exert its pressure. It is both impossible and necessary and therefore its fulfilment can only be by grace and faithfulness, never by effort and success.

'Damian' was a student at university who died young of an inoperable cancer. He had a deep sense of vocation to ordained ministry and other people had affirmed this. He found it hard to accept that, despite everything he had learned, not least in his illness, his hopes were not to be fulfilled. I wrote him a letter at the time, trying to set out what I believed to be a true perspective, however difficult it might be to embrace it. This is the substance of that letter.

"Damian, perhaps you are already what you want to be – 'God's priest'. And I don't mean that glibly or in such a way as to deny the loss and pain. And it's not simply that you belong to the priesthood of all believers – though that is true – but that this is true for you more profoundly than it is for most people much older than you are. You've given so much in your short life, much love and wisdom and skill, not least with your music and your friendships. And I know it's not been easy. You had a hard time of it early on, and somehow you've been determined not to give back evil for evil. It's cost you a lot – more, it seems, than you can bear, our common fragility having come home to you sooner than to most of us. But you've not stopped loving, even through the suffering of this illness. I suppose it has something to do with the narrow way, the eye of the needle that, humanly speaking, is impossible to get through. But you're offering it – or at least some of it – in love for the healing of others. Remember that it was said of Jesus, with mockery yet with more truth than they realized, He saved others; himself he cannot save. And *that's* what *makes* a priest. You don't have to worry in the end whether you're 'ordained' or not. In the quality of your living and dying you're there already."

So the Christian vocation is

to *die and rise with Christ:* this is the pattern of our living, focused for us at the beginning in our Baptism, renewed in each Eucharist, fulfilled in the smallest of selfless deeds;

to be *a member of the Body of Christ,* a living organism in which each cell is vital to the well-being of the whole;

to live this life of Love in a mobile, fragmented, rapidly changing, complex urban society, *exercising gifts of ministry* at home, at work, in the community – gifts of listening, of knowledge, of insight, of caring, of skill, of encouragement, of hospitality;

to *respond simply and truthfully* as each occasion demands, much more than to make a high-powered articulate commitment; to have the sense of quiet self-value and worth that comes from deeply believing that God has been shown to us in Jesus, that God wants us to follow Jesus, to belong to the People of God, to pray and worship and serve;

to *serve in humble ways,* knowing that this counts with God as much as if not more than ministering in the limelight, and so refusing to turn the not-so-bright and the not-so-able into second class Christians just because they can't take on more public responsibilities.

To serve –
it is the way of 'deaconing',
of the one who waits at table,
and does the job best when least noticed. .

It is the way of the Jesus who said
he was among us as one who serves...

The servant community that is the Church
has no place for thrones, lords, and domination,
only for tables and chairs, water and towels,
bread and wine, the good book and good friends,
no place for anything that obscures the truth
that the child, the outcast, the failure
are the ones who are closest to God's heart.

Live from and with the child within you,
the rejected, the insignificant, the failure,
yes, within you and among you,
and you will bear the indelible mark
of the Suffering Servant,
without which you cannot be recognized
as an authentic follower.

Live the life of the Suffering Servant,
in and through the ordinary and the everyday,
suffering for truth and conscience
or because of physical or emotional damage,
quietly serving others with no recognition.

There is no other genuine qualification
for any ministry which entrusts you with power...

2

Hidden People:
Being present incognito

IF we are called be a priestly people, to minister in ways of humble service in the Spirit of the self-giving love of Christ, then it is worth asking this question,

> How have I ministered to others, and how have others ministered to me, in hidden, obscure, even secret ways?

It is not easy to answer that question because we should expect *not* to notice when these things are happening. Nevertheless, it is worth pondering...

A hidden people...

Hiddenness and secrecy have always been marks of the story of the People of God, not least in times of persecution. One of the earliest Christian 'secret signs' of recognition, still to be seen scratched on the walls of the catacombs in Rome, was that of the fish. In Greek it is spelt 'ichthus', the letters of which are the first letters of the words in the phrase, 'Jesus Christ, Son of God, Saviour'.

High walls of protection and a measure of secrecy, away from the glare of publicity, are needed when a relationship or a project or a community are young and vulnerable. We should expect not to hear too much of new life in the Church, stirring in small and hidden cells, germinating slowly, far from great occasions in large buildings and arenas — especially when the latter look as if they are too akin to displays of earthly power and glory.

Think of the hidden ministry of small groups of people who have been inspired by the Taizé Community in France. Scattered all over the world, yet held together by a common loyalty to the Gospel, they are acting as seemingly insignificant yeast in inner cities, racial ghettoes, and tired parishes. Joining them may be those who have left the traditional religious communities because they have become too powerful, public, and institutionalised.

Among the hidden will be those who need never be concerned to lock their doors at night.

In his novel, *Incognito,* Petru Dumitriu describes a hidden world beneath the outer one of oppressive government and secret police. In the crowded streets of the city he would exchange a glance, a few words, even a silence, and know that he was not alone. There is a 'dense and secret undergrowth which is wholly composed of personal events.'[10]

Incognito, silent, simple, obscure, secret: perhaps it is all part of the right hand not knowing what the left is doing, so sly and shy is it in its actions. A vein of hiddenness needs to run through every Christian life, especially in those who exercise public office. If we possess any kind of wealth – of money or talent or power – then we need to be pruned, made to realize what the poor and oppressed already know, that we give most genuinely and selflessly out of what we lack. For the successful and independent this is a hard saying. But as deprived, useless, as nothing... yet making many rich...

❖

A hidden God...

The story is told of a grey-bearded distinguished-looking principal of a theological college. He was attending a social function at a psychiatric hospital. A man came up to him and addressed him as God. He replied that he was incognito and never discussed business outside office hours.

> After the presence, an absence...
> After the revelation, a hiding...
> After the obvious, the obscure...

It was Job's experience of God, echoed by all of us at one time or another:

I go forward but he is not there,
and backward but I cannot perceive him.
On the left hand I seek him,
but I cannot behold him,
I turn to the right hand
but I cannot see him.[11]

A God incognito and unrecognized...
Hidden in Jesus of Nazareth...
Among you stands one whom you do not know...
The wounded one beyond recognition on the Cross...
Their eyes were kept from recognizing him...

A French Roman Catholic – I think it was Péguy – found himself saying that the purpose of his ministry in this day and age was 'to keep the rumour of God alive'.

A hidden self...

Because each of us is unfathomably mysterious and unique, so not one of us can escape the journey into our deeper, often hidden self and the encounter with loneliness and despair – often in a place where God "is more absent than a dead man, more absent than light in the utter darkness of a cell..."[12] It is the place of meeting with those parts of ourselves that we would prefer not to have to recognize and love. It is also a place of meeting with the crucified God. We may not expect there to be such a meeting, but sometimes we refuse to recognize the Presence at the very point where we are hiding from ourselves.

In the secret place we are given a new identity and a new name:

> "I will give to the one who conquers a white
> stone, with a new name written on the stone,
> known only to the one who receives it."[13]

The white stone is a symbol of integration, of the weaving of the various strands of our personality, with their varied hues, into a whole pattern, focused on Christ.

Our eyes need to be sharpened in order to see God in dark places, in others and in ourselves, wherever we human beings take faltering steps in our confusions. For all of us time is needed, a refining of the dross far from the public eye. For without such a hidden process public ministry becomes arrogant, a loving of the limelight as an escape from the acid dark.

Think of...

> the contemplative monk or nun in an enclosed community behind high walls;

> the urban hermit obscurely present on a raw housing estate;

> an explorer on a psychotherapeutic journey;

> a bereaved woman who has worked through grief and become a sign of love-in-solitude, of loneliness transformed into a wider loving and a deeper compassion;

> a man who lives from the inside of his lack of love, from the within of hollow ache, and gives unselfishly from that very place.

3
Dispersed People:
Actively engaging with the secular

THE general context of ministry is this:
The whole People of God, ministering in
the Spirit of Love, being 'priestly',
'deaconing', often incognito.

The *place* of that ministry for most Christian people is some part
of the secular world. And the first demand of that ministry is that
we do as well as we are able that which we have to do. Such work
for the common good is our proper and significant contribution
to be valued equally with – if not more – than any contribution
we might also make to the life of the Church. Dorothy Sayers
thought it both a waste of energy and even a sacrilege to deflect
people from the secular into the ecclesiastical.[14]

We are to think of ourselves, not as isolated individuals but as
part of a variety of communities and associations. We may live
in a culture which is individualistic, but we are called to be
persons-in-community.

Rather more specifically and emerging from this background,
we become aware of ourselves as the scattered People of God,
dispersed as individuals and as groups, in places of politics,
industry, business, communications, etc. awakening to new
dimensions of ministry that have often been ignored. To say that
being a Christian at work is only a matter of being honest and
doing one's job competently is to miss the significance of our
participation in corporate, institutional life, in the very way its
affairs are conducted. We are, each and every one of us,
connected in an intricate web of organisations which have a
strong influence. Think of the power of the multinationals, of
new means of communication, of shifting patterns of 'employment'. (It is a sign of the times to need to put that word in
inverted commas.). Think too of the ethical dilemmas, not

19

least in commerce and medicine, which afford no straight-forward solutions. To be a thoughtful and committed Christian in such circumstances cannot be easy.

> So a further question suggests itself:
> What might be the spiritual disciplines
> and mutual support needed to sustain a
> vision of God's reign and the hope of
> its coming on earth?

An American Christian writes:

> "... my basic frustration is that I can't see anywhere in the Church a recognition of, or much support for, my ministry as an engineer in a large corporation. I've come to think of it as an invisible ministry, not only to the church, but also to myself most of the time. It's a difficult and lonely ministry at best, but even more so because generally it isn't even seen as a valid ministry at all, or at least that's my impression."[15]

Is the Church unconcerned?

What and who in this context is the Church? Only the Sunday congregation or the vicar saying Grace at the firm's annual dinner?

Are ordinary people "either lost in the world or trapped in the Church"?[16]

Is it impossible to be a Christian at work because you have to compromise too much?

Is the world of factory and office a godless place, God's Presence there being limited to a few individual Christians?

Or is the Presence of God more subtly to be discerned in and amongst the life of factory and office, waiting to be listened to and celebrated?

Is a significant part of ministering the Gospel a dialogue with the people, concerns, and institutions of secular life?

If so, how might the People of God equip one another for that dialogue?

"What is needed is the active presence in factories and workplaces of pioneers who are fully conscious of their double vocation – as Christians and as workers – and who are bent on assuming their responsibilities to the full, knowing neither peace nor rest until they have transformed the environment of their lives to the demands of the Gospel."[17]

This is not to deny godlessness, even though we might differ in where we 'locate' it. Indeed, study of the New Testament involves discerning when 'world' means 'the whole of God's creation' and when it means 'as organized against the will of God'. There has always been a tension between the two. Dietrich Bonhoeffer saw more deeply than most the challenge presented by a supposedly godless world. He drew a distinction between the 'religious' attitude which encourages us in our weakness and distress to look to the power of God to rescue us from the world and the biblical revelation of God's powerlessness and suffering at the hands of godlessness. He goes on to emphasize that Christians must really *live* in that place without as it were creating a religious ghetto, really live a 'secular' life and so share the suffering of God.[18]

Consequently a 'priestly' life is as costly and sacrificial in the 'world' as it is in the 'church' – probably more so.

A banker was struggling to keep a firm going when closure would have meant the loss of a thousand jobs. At the same time he recognized his responsibility to those who had invested their savings in the bank. Inevitably he was caught up in compromises and at first he thought it was no use continuing to claim to be a Christian. But a number of things happened:

> He became a member of a support group which included other Christian financiers. He experienced affirmation from others.

> He reflected more deeply on the meaning of his work and began to see that the world of money was not by definition separated from God. To evaluate its place you needed to take into account attitude and use.

> Having at one time thought that to be Christian was to be 'righteous', he came to understand the call to be 'faithful', and to have the courage to act and to know oneself forgiven.

> He began to discern God's presence in his work and to understand that it is "only by plunging into the life of the world that one learns how to believe."[9]

> He saw that it is possible to make changes for good, but only if you co-operate with others.

Another businessman reported experiencing spiritual growth even when skirting bankruptcy. He had worked for twenty-five years in his family building firm. For the first fifteen of those years he had seen his job solely as a means of feeding and clothing his family. Then control of the business passed to him and he began expanding and diversifying.

At this time be began another kind of journey. A churchgoer since his youth, he had served in a variety of traditional roles. But he now joined a group which was alive not only to prayer and study of the Bible but also to the possibilities that come from sharing feelings and concerns at a deep level. He began to know, rather than just know about, trust and forgiveness.

His business was affected by a recession and he contemplated getting out and seeking to be accepted for the ministry of leadership in his church. Instead, with the group's support, he sold off a majority of his business interests and consolidated round a single specialised function. In order to cope with the stress he began to keep a regular time of solitude and developed a daily discipline of prayer and keeping a journal. He now reads from the entries of previous years and keeps track of where he is going.

As the discipline took root, so did a sense of ministry on the job. He calls it a ministry of affirmation. Much of his time is spent going round building sites, meeting with contractors and suppliers, and he has them in mind in his morning prayers, seeking to become sensitive to their needs.

At the same time a larger vision of the business is taking shape as he finds a connection between his work and his understanding of God. He tries to convey to his workers the importance of the fact that they are constructing someone's living or working environment, that people will spend hours a day in the space they provide. He tries to be both conscientious and thankful about this, even finding he enjoys payday. He realises that it is not only a responsibility but a way of affirming everyone's contribution when he pays a just wage cheerfully.[20]

Geoffrey Lampe reflected in a more theologically sustained way on this kind of experience and struggle. He showed how the idea of priesthood applied in fact not only to believers – and certainly not only to clergy – but to the whole of humankind. God commissions and empowers human beings to become what they are intended to become, the 'true Adam', Christlike – people who declare the wisdom and will of God and become channels of God's love and care for the whole of creation.

That is one central idea about priesthood, one direction of movement. The other key idea is that human beings should represent the creation in responding to, moving towards, praising God – no longer by animal sacrifices but by being consecrated for sacrificial living – and serving God's creative purposes. Again this is to be like Christ, who embodied this dedication to God.

So God has called the people of Israel into covenant, to become priests mediating God to the peoples of the world and the peoples of the world to God. This mission was fulfilled by Jesus, representing both Adam and Israel. The Spirit of Jesus empowers the community of his followers to be a true Israel, a priestly community, again representing humanity in its Godward dedication and communicating God to humankind as a channel of the divine love.[21]

How then can business people become and encourage others to become 'priestly' people?

Locating Ministries
on the Boundary
of Society and Church

4

Pioneering People:
Exploring beyond the known

WE are called to serve one another in the Spirit of Sacrificial Love, sometimes simply being prayerfully present to others, the world, and God, sometimes incognito, sometimes dispersed throughout society, responding to whatever opportunities present themselves in the world of which we are a part.

There will also be some who find themselves serving in unexpected places, beyond the boundaries of the familiar. They are the ones who are particularly aware that we have no abiding city, that we are continually being called to venture, like Abraham, into the unknown, in faith.

This is our 'apostolic' ministry: we are a people who are *sent*, who are *compelled to go*, like the apostles of old, seeking to understand the 'language' of the new places and people and occasions and to bring to light, to 'reveal' whatever of the Gospel we find there or is waiting to be shown there – in words fresh-minted, in deeds as yet hidden.

There are some – the shy artists who need well-protected places – who exercise this ministry in private ways, others who are recognized more publicly to be so doing. Even the artists may be among them when they can dare the risk of sharing what they have heard and seen.

When the frontier of the familiar is closed...

We live in a time of fresh thinking about issues of human sexuality and gender in the context of Christian love and ministry. The People of God as a whole are uncertain whether or not to authorize some of their number to public office – women, lesbian and gay people, divorced people. We are living with this question,

27

> Should some ways of ministering be closed to people
> on grounds of gender, sexual preference, or failure
> of a relationship?

More particularly, those who are affected personally in these
ways have to ask themselves the question,

> How may God be calling me to minister when certain
> frontiers are closed to me?

A student on a theological training course was deeply disturbed
by some sessions on the themes of Guilt and Penitence. In one
way she had always known that in present circumstances she
could not be an 'ordained' minister, exercising the ministry of
leadership, but she suddenly became deeply aware how limiting
it would be not to be able to focus her pastoral work in formally
administering the Sacrament of Reconciliation, and, in the
name of God, absolving the penitent.

A frontier was closed to her. Did this mean that she had to wait
for 'them' to change the rules? Could she perhaps perceive two
challenges to wrestle with?

The first is to work for a change in church policy and canon
law, to try and hasten the day when women will be treated on
equal terms with men in the ministry of leadership.

The second is to use the energy locked in frustration to dig
more deeply into her understanding and practice of forgiveness
to see whether there might be something new to be discovered
that could be shared with the whole church, just as the first
apostles had something new about salvation to offer to their
fellow Jews – however costly such pioneering, ancient and
modern, is bound to be.

Then there are some further questions that might be asked
along the way:

Is authority to absolve given by Jesus only to certain
representative individuals or to the People of God as a whole?
Can a person be so set 'apart' from the body that he or she is no
longer 'a part' of the body?

Is it an inner law of relationships that all of us have the power over one another to bind and release?

Might it be the first concern of the leader of the community to teach about, to encourage, to stimulate the dynamic of forgiveness rather than to exercise an exclusive power?

And so on. The point here is not to find an easy resolution of that particular issue, but to recognize that the person who cannot walk in familiar territory is compelled to live elsewhere, searching, raising questions, learning new languages. All this is vital to the well-being of those back home, however unwelcome and disturbing travellers' tales may be. And if you are called to be 'apostolic', 'missionary', you cannot exercise that ministry from the centre, but only from the edge – though not off the edge, for that would be to lose touch altogether and have no opportunity of sharing what has been learned.

Notice that this was the experience of the apostles, whose 'home-base' was Jewish and whom God 'sent' to the Gentiles. (The fact that the Church soon lost touch with its home-base and forgot the rock whence it was hewn is one of the tragedies of history that is only now beginning to be redeemed.)

'To be sent', 'to be compelled' – the phrases are almost synonymous. Sometimes we use the word 'compel' in the context of a lack of freedom, but in the strange way in which opposites belong together, places of compulsion or necessity can in time become places of freedom. For example, we can respond to limitations or inescapable demands with self-pity and bitterness, or we can see those conditions of necessity as exactly the place of God's presence and challenge and the opportunity for growth and freedom. Abraham was sent – or was he compelled? – to go forth from his father's house. The Book of Common Prayer points us to God whose service is perfect freedom.

This suggests that the human grounding of God's call, God's sending out of men and women, is an odd mixture of motive and personal circumstance and family history. Perhaps it is God's habit to use all that is unresolved in us in ways that turn out to be for others' greater good as well as for our own.

External circumstances may also be part of this human ground of apostolicity. For we may find a growing concern within, something that is 'laid upon us' that we know that we must not avoid. We may find ourselves drawn to – or is it sent to? – people and places of deprivation, sometimes 'over there', where God is waiting to be revealed, sometimes 'in here', in the depths of our own being, where a new face of God is waiting to be revealed, often hidden in the very pain of the deprivation. There will always be places where God has not yet been named, and it will always be a risk to go there.

Vincent Donovan has used the phrase 'social martyrs'[22] to describe missionaries, for they are cut off from their cultural and social roots, strangers in a strange land. Does this indicate that the best missionaries in our own society will be drawn from among ethnic minorities, women, and gay and lesbian people?

Remember that this 'sentness', this love that 'compels', is focused on the movement of Love that is God risking all in the Incarnation. God never plays safe. And in that 'moving Spirit', the Spirit of death-defeating Love, the first apostles were caught up, sent into foreign territory, beyond the familiar, to places of Greek language and culture. They were not sure in advance how Jewish those Gentiles would have to become in order to be followers of the Way. The result is recorded in the Acts of the Apostles, in words that often sound muted now but must have been white-hot at the time.

The apostle, the missionary, the evangelist of today, the pioneer for God, has to become a crucible out of which burning words and deeds will come that will convict and convince. They may be heard and seen in public. But there are also the lonelier ones, the artists, who are compelled to be creators before their time of images that will speak of God in the future. In either case, a man or woman will gradually or suddenly recognize 'the call' and know that their lives must be centred round their response to it.[23] To be 'apostolic' becomes the *characteristic* stance of certain people, first in their own eyes and then tested out before others.

At first, the 'evangelist' or the 'poet' will tentatively 'taste' their 'name'. They may need others to convince them that it is their true name – or that they have been mistaken. On occasion they may recognize their call only when another has named them. But from that moment on they know that they will be denying the truth and betraying their Creator if they ignore their name.

It may seem strange that 'evangelist' and 'poet' are put together as variants of 'missionary' or 'apostle'. But the world is a poorer place for there being evangelists who lack imagination and poets who lack recognition.

So there is paradox, the *one* truth in *both*

> gift and talent;
> destiny and freedom;
> divine and human;
> call and choice.

Go deep into that which you are aware of and you will find yourself caught up into much more than you can possibly be aware of.

Reflect for yourself on these things. Ask if any of it resonates in the kind of way that might be indicating to you that here is your characteristic way of being in the world. Here are two lists of words, descriptions to use in order to test your 'location'. (The typist wondered if that was a misprint for 'vocation'.)

Edges	Centre
Pioneer	Settler
Frontiers	Homeland
Wilderness	Village, town, or city
The new	The old
Nonconformist	Conformist
Experimenter	Conserver
Irritant	Diplomat
Discoverer	Archivist
Fool	King
Clown	Ringmaster
Midwife	Mother
Traveller	Home-maker

[That these images are mostly masculine indicates that this particular set of opposites is not absolute. There may be an unexamined mindset at work which needs questioning. At the very least we might ask how there might be communication between the opposites in such a way as to bring them more happily together.]

❖

All this is to suggest that the work of 'evangelists' is not as obvious and clearcut as some would suppose. The words of the preacher should be like those of the poet – mysterious, challenging, compelling. The patterns of worship and community life should not be fossilized but should at least hint at ways that will be strange to those already settled. This is perhaps but to remind ourselves that there has always been tension between the Church as continuing institution and the Church as mission, requiring the flexibility of response that institutions can rarely give.

So if this 'pioneering', 'apostolic', 'evangelistic', 'missionary' way of ministering becomes the *characteristic* concern of certain members of the body, they are not likely to find themselves at ease within an institutional framework nor will the institution be at ease with them. Bishops may have blessed missionaries who go conveniently far away, but they are not always noted for their enthusiasm in supporting experiments nearer home – especially if they provoke controversy or show every likelihood of failure. But experimenters cannot experiment without more licence than usually appears on licences. A mature Church might more readily commission apostles and pioneers, encouraging them with wisdom, sending them forth, and giving them room to breathe.

For the sending forth these days is not so much to distant fields as to pastures and cities nearer home, to the complexities of urban societies, and to the mysterious depths of the human psyche – all places where there is rarely much room to breathe. The mission 'field' is now the shopping mall, the sports complex, the business house, and is not just to individuals who happen to be there, but to the complicated corporate life of the institutions concerned and how they relate to financiers, councillors, government, and local community. Alas that mission in an industrial diocese often has a harder time justifying its share of the budget than the committee that looks after churches and vicarages.

There is always the need for groups and individuals to take courage and freedom into their own hands and to work without official approval or blessing or even recognition. It takes courage to risk and probably to fail. If we do not ourselves make room for our own work, waiting for others to clear a path for us, we may not be worthy of freedom.[24]

John Drury reminds us of three angular figures who yet made significant contributions to the life of the Church: Søren Kierkegaard who sat in his club on Sunday mornings, Charles Péguy, a lonely figure who was never comfortably at home in the Church, and Simone Weil, who believed deeply yet refused to be baptized. Awkward as they are, we would be the poorer without them.[25]

More formally, the World Council of Churches' report, *Baptism, Eucharist, and Ministry,* affirms that 'new impulses' have often had to find their way into the life of the Church by 'unusual ways'.[26] But after a while the more cautious, those 'back home', may be impressed sufficiently by a few of these experiments as to say — as did the Council of Jerusalem in the early days of the Church about the Mission to the Gentiles, "Yes, this is authentic, it carries conviction. Its authority is growing. It is within the apostolic tradition." To reach that point of recognition, to become an integrated part of the whole Church, may indeed be the intention of the experimenter. But there is often the need to be apart for a while, to learn what that contribution may be, to test it out, and to wait in the wings.

Perhaps, too, those of us who are called to pioneer need to be careful not to expect the whole Church quickly to move to where we are. Edward Schillebeeckx allows generously for the authenticity of 'critical communities' but points out that a change which does not commend itself to the vast majority of Christian people will simply produce new schisms. Such communities have the necessary function of stimulus and ferment, often from the margins, so that the whole Church can become ripe for the introduction of what they have pioneered.[27]

❖

I wonder if it has been the basic calling of religious communities of monks and nuns to be apostolic pioneers, either in places of 'poverty' in the outer world or in inner places of 'poverty' within themselves, living lives of contemplation and simplicity, unexpectedly discovering and being discovered there by God.

'Jean' wasn't one particular person, but a kind of composite portrait of a few people I have been privileged to know...

She was a special person. Goodness shone out of her – though she never hid her faults and you knew she stood with the same foot of clay as you do. It's just that you felt that she walked with God, and you always came away refreshed from having been with her. She made sacrifice look lovely, not harsh. Somehow the commitment she had made more than fifty years ago started her on a way of life that transformed her. I suppose she let the love and light of God into far more of the dark places than most of us ever dare to do. Yet she never lost touch with her own or others' earthiness, nor with the tortuous ways of human life. You knew that she'd been there already – how, you never knew but didn't need to – and she had not been overwhelmed. She did nothing that we can't do, but she gave you the courage to set out again on the way. Without people like her, most of us would never take any steps at all. She was one of God's specially chosen people, living at the boundaries of what we could all become. She was there, not instead of us, but on our behalf. People like her refuse to let us keep our slippers on. And if somehow we don't follow or if they themselves refuse, then God has to work longer at redeeming our tragedies and transforming them into love.

The titles 'minister-at-work' or 'minister in secular employment' sound like hazard signs at the edge of the road – or at least an unusual phenomenon if seen on a weekday. But it is a common title now for another group of pioneers who are doing something a bit more public than ministering as individuals in a hidden or dispersed way. Yet they are not as ecclesiastical as Industrial Chaplains (see chapter 5). They are recognized and authorized by the Church to minister while continuing in secular employment. Such people often feel they are living on a frontier, yet able to discover-uncover the presence of God there, and given the opportunity to articulate that on behalf of the Church.

Other titles are used for this ministry: non-stipendiary, self-supporting, auxiliary, assistant, worker-priest – and even hedge-priest! The variety and uncertainty are good indications that we are in pioneering territory.

Immediately we recognize tensions. If the Church commissions certain of its members with the specific understanding that they will remain in their secular employment and pioneer a visible Christian presence while contributing with their skills to the life of that institution (like the 'worker priests' in France), does this de-value, dis-enable, the more hidden ministries of those who are dispersed more generally throughout society? We are moving away from those ministries which can be exercised without anybody waiting for 'permission': they belong to all who are baptised. And we are moving towards those ministries where a few are in some sense recognized and authorized to be 'representatives' of the Church. Is there really a need for this?

However, it is a fact of life that the individual Christian does not sense a representative responsibility of accountability either to the Church or to the workplace, beyond the individual contribution a practising Christian is already making. Moreover, we live in an age when we spend more and more of our time as members of complex corporate bodies, and communication between them is by means of representatives. Such institutions and associations are at least as important as the geographical neighbourhood of our homes. Symbolic persons may be of value in each of these places, not just in the residential neighbourhood. Then and only then will they come to believe that the Church is committed to affirming them and ministering among them – precisely because it is committed publicly and corporately.

But can we have a representative of a Christian community in a place where there is no such community? Well, there are doubtless individual Christians scattered there already, concerned very much with profound questions of ethics, and might they not be helped by encouragement and inspiration from someone like themselves who is committed to the same place of work with all its ambiguities and opportunities and who, unlike themselves, is called to a more public profile of their faith? Such public figures may be akin to those missionaries who worked for years building up relationships in a new 'society', exercising a ministry of presence and sometimes of prophetic critique, before there could be any sense of a Christian community as leaven or as gathered for worship. Such a 'church' would at most be latent, not yet able to recognize itself, through the focal, representative person as part of a wider Church.

Moreover, there is something new going on in the world today. For the local vicar is neither the 'persona' of the village where everybody is baptised (as in medieval 'Christendom') nor the pastor of an independent congregation that has separated itself from what it believes to be 'the wicked world'. The world is not the enemy nor is the Church the place of the pure. In a more complex society we need two-footed, two-eyed people who are convinced of the need to focus life on God *and* convinced that God is waiting already to be revealed, uncovered, in the minute particulars of the everyday secular world. This does not mean identifying with the current powers that be, nor absenting oneself from them. Encouragement and criticism can belong together in a mature organisation.

So we might discern the need for significant people at significant points of overlap, incognito and engaged Christians, yes, but representative ones too, those who know both 'church' and 'organisation' well. If this is not happening, the Church is in danger of being a place of nostalgia and escape, occasionally flickering with life but to most human beings as harmless and irrelevant as flat-earthers. The other danger is that the Church sets itself up to be the ideal society, with all the right answers to all the questions, taking its embattled place against all the other clashing -isms and ideologies, each a closed system that promises life but delivers death.

'David' is a maintenance electrician in a large pharmaceutical company. The nature of his job enables him to go anywhere in the factory and be on easy terms with people in different departments. He has a given base from which to build up a network of people at least interested in spiritual questions, across the boundaries of workers, management, and unions. They meet from time to time to eat and talk, trying to discern what God is up to in the works and seeing what it might mean to align themselves with God's purposes. David sees this as a kind of hallowing of the workplace, an encouraging of others to practise their priestly ministry to the whole created world. He also convenes a Deanery Group for Church and Industry. They are concerned for example with the problems of workers from ethnic minorities. And he occasionally preaches in church, largely telling the stories of the Gospel that have occurred at his place of work. And he tries to suggest new patterns of prayer and spiritual discipline within the setting of work.

'Barbara' also works in a factory, in the personnel department. She sees her ministry in a slightly different way from David, more pastoral, more to individuals. She asks what qualities are demanded of her, and she thinks of patience, endurance, listening; trying to bind the wounds in the factory, sewing torn nets together again; hinting at possibilities of co-operation in a competitive atmosphere; being aware of others at the boundaries where one group bumps into another.

'Roger' is a teacher who wrote this short piece for the Newsletter of Ministers-at-Work: "I keep going, refreshed by such moments as when the fifth year stopped smoking and drinking for two weeks and collected £85 for Dr Barnardo's. It was just before Christmas . . . and a kind of birth came about in all our hearts, a birth that convinced me that many people are very close to God and that the Kingdom is something to strive for still as we live together on earth – so near – yet so far – but *there* in Christ."[28]

'Paul', writing for the same magazine, specifically uses the image of the pioneer: "Inevitably, during the pioneering time we are not so much the new born children of a new ministry, as everybody else's rusk. People embedded in the existing ecclesiastical and secular structures will cut their teeth on us. That is very much what we are for and where we should be. (The fact that we are not clearly definable is) inevitable for pioneers who are always pushing beyond the limits of existing experiences."[29]

'Alan' is seeking to be ordained, though he often wonders why. He sees little connection in practice between church on Sunday and his work in training the unskilled for new jobs – let alone his trade union responsibilities. He does not see his ministry as that of a vicar, but feels that his being ordained will open doors that would otherwise stay firmly shut. He thinks this has something to do with a folklore of men of integrity and honesty – though he also remembers other clergy who don't at all give that impression. And he believes that for the time being he has simply to be a bit more obvious in the factory as a Christian and hope for a way in which he can be known as accountable to the Church and representing it.

'Peter' wrote in a report on his first term of training for ordained ministry: "The disappointment for me was that so many students still see ministry solely or predominantly in parochial terms and are not wanting to explore the wider implications of Christianity and ministry in the secular world. I would be happier if more students intended to stay in the secular world they know rather than escaping – if that is not too strong a word – into a parish church."[30]

I recall coming across this quotation some years ago, I think in the *Church Times,* from an experienced vicar. I hope he won't mind being quoted here: "In commuter parishes there are whole streets empty all day of parishioners who are at work; who ministers to them? Is it the incumbent... or the non-stipendiary minister sharing the same bench or desk?"

Michael Ranken, a food technologist, recognizes that his ministry is a missionary task. Therefore he has to learn the language of the people among whom he moves. He realizes that he cannot expect to communicate through the symbols "under which the 'home' Church describes and handles her vision."[31] Further, he expects to find symbols and perceptions wherever he goes in the secular world, however strange these may seem. "For God... reveals himself as he always has and to whom he pleases, when and how he chooses. We must not suppose that the Church contains the only ones to have noticed."

There is a message here to those who minister from within the Church as institution. They are not going to be the ones who directly hear the accents of God in the many complex 'languages' of the world today. But to affirm those who can and in turn to listen to them are vital tasks. Such listening demands time and patience, an acute ear, and an unusual humility.

"... consider the sewage worker, the dustman, the morgue attendant, the lavatory paper manufacturer, and their share in keeping us healthy, each continually recognizing, acknowledging, accepting, correcting faults – and forgiving them, for in the world 'out there' not so many of the myriad errors that they face are actually left unresolved, provoking guilt ... note how much of good 'secular' management techniques attend to the business of bringing errors to light, gently, so that they can be resolved and new life begin. And the sewage worker and the others are doing God's work for us (or is it our work for God) with real sacrifice of social regard. They work, by the large, as God does, silently and without thanks. By the rest of us, by and large, they are misunderstood, disparaged, or ignored. And the work of giving, of creating life, goes on. They are our servants. Isaiah's descriptions fit. Daily they forgive our negligencies and ignorances, mostly they do not store them up or hold them against us. That is much more than we deserve, and in that respect too we should see that it is exactly what we say about God."[32]

❖

And he also says this:

"I have argued that repentance and forgiveness, being God's properties, are also properties of all well run carpenters' shops. We are to mediate them as they occur, promote them when they are deficient. We must be expected to be entrusted with confessions of a somewhat different order from those which a parish priests hears, of technical, commercial, or even corporation errors. We have the Church's authority to pronounce absolution to the penitent; at work we have also the authority which comes of true knowledge of the issues. Of course we are to intercede for, to bless, to teach and encourage those with whom we work, both people and systems. And when projects, systems or organisations are sick or dying they too need this ministry of someone who loves and knows them."[33]

And what of the common people who heard Jesus gladly? Have the poor and the oppressed (whether linguistically, emotionally, economically, politically, sexually), those who are pressed down with burdens imposed by others – have these people ever known what it is to say, "Now we hear the wonderful works of God *in our own language*"? Most of them are not members of local churches and many of them have no work. When will the Church authorize and support some of its members to "sit where they sit"? Who will represent the voiceless and give them a voice – or, better, enable them to *speak* in their own language?[34] Perhaps, of course, there are a few, working away quietly, like the Little Sisters and Brothers of Jesus, who work in menial jobs and who pray and who are hospitable, and who are sometimes cherished by the Church and sometimes ignored . . .

Here are some 'apostolic metaphors', some images to play with in the imagination. They may or may not resonate. You may or may not be in the process of 'locating' yourself here.

Clowns:

> Useless parasites on society, with no obvious role, adding nothing to the Gross National Product, a standing affront to those who judge by wealth or status.

> Disturbers of the peace, uncomfortable if they come too close, with a painted face masking you know not what. Is this encounter going to work out for my good?

> The court jesters who are the only ones allowed to tell the king unpleasant truths, getting away with it because they have no ambition for power, casting

doubt on old certainties, ridiculing conventional wisdoms, discovering truths in the absurd.

Outcasts who are often sent to sleep in the kennels or put in the stocks, at home with the debris and dregs, with the clumsy, the awkward, the dis-graced, themselves without social graces, yet at the moment of emptiness the ones who are filled with grace, thoroughly at home anywhere on earth, never really exiled, the only true citizens.

Irrepressible fools who bounce back for more, resurrection showing up death for the joke it is, voices merry with the laughter that is our saving grace.

Entertainers at the Great Banquet. Ah, but wait. At this Feast the King comes down from the throne, for he is himself the clown for his guests – or rather the Clown of clowns, Fool of fools, the only Entertainer of Jesters.

Indelible Markers

A special people, marked indelibly, not as with a magic marker, but because it is impossible as the years go by to erase the marks of a vow or promise, either in your own or in other people's lives.

This is true even if you fail to grow into the promise – or in some sense grow beyond it, for there are always those in each generation who are called to leave one commitment for the sake of another, however unknown and dangerous the path. They may have to go beyond the regular life of church and society precisely for the sake of that church and that society – for God's good purposes.

Whether you faithfully stay or faithfully move on, the mark is still there. It will be etched in the body. It will make you for ever a different person. It will reveal to you who you are. It has something of the eternal about it – though you will not have been transported into a realm not inhabited by ordinary mortals. No, it is more about a transfiguration. It has something to do with Light – and even with haloes. It can be recognized in the lines of a face, in a look of the eyes, in wounds of hands and feet, in a limp that reminds you of a wrestling with God. It is the mark of the baptised, it is the birthmark of reborn humanity.

The mark may remain hidden – or it may become clear. But only the indelibly marked, whose mark has been recognized, can become those who focus our human concern for ultimate things, can become stewards of the mysteries of God. They take to themselves the world's odium, its cry of rage against a God who seems so cruel, and against a Church whose members have so often betrayed humankind, with inquisitions and bibliolatry, communicating a stern and destructive God who is supposed to be highly selective in the giving of love and life. They take to themselves the projections of those who cannot face their own darknesses, they are absorbers of the world's pain. They transform it by allowing it to enter their hearts and meet there the Spirit of transforming love. And they receive the deepest mark of all, the indelible mark of laughter and joy.

Like Teilhard de Chardin, they want to be "the first to become conscious of all that the world loves, pursues, and suffers, the first to open themselves out and sacrifice themselves, to become more widely human and more nobly of the earth than any of the world's servants."[36]

Star Throwers

The naturalist Loren Eiseley, in an essay called *The Star Thrower*,[37] describes the beaches of Costabel on the Atlantic coast of America. They attract shipwrecks. Gulls cut to pieces the hermit crabs thrown up by the sea. Starfish suffocate because their pores become blocked by sand. Collectors, using electric torches in the hours before dawn, seek shells whose inhabitants will tickle the palates of tourists in the hotels.

In the midst of this death and desolation, there is a strange man who walks by the sea and throws starfish back into the water. He reckons they may live if the offshore pull is strong enough.

Eiseley can at first make no sense of it. His life at the time reflected the events of the beach, dominated as it was by gloom and defeat. Yet, he writes, "I turned as I neared a bend in the

coast, and saw him toss another star, skimming it skilfully far out
over the ravening and tumultuous water. For a moment, in the
changing light, the sower appeared magnified, as though casting
larger stars upon some greater sea. He had, at any rate, the
posture of a god."[38]

Gradually the image works its way into the depths of his being,
through the thick layers of his bleak, death-dealing materialism,
until he realizes that "through war and famine and death, a
sparse mercy had persisted, like a mutation whose time had not
yet come."[39]

It is rumoured among some that Christ was that mutation and
that a few are called in each generation to keep that rumour alive.
For its time, if intimated, even inaugurated, has not yet come to
fruition. There has been one who has walked through a place of
a skull, into a tomb of rock, and out into a garden.

Eiseley goes on to join the star thrower on the beach. For there
had been kindled within him a faint memory of compassion.
"Somewhere, my thought persisted, there is a hurler of stars, and
he walks, because he chooses, always in desolation, but not in
defeat."[40]

Thresholds and Porches

Some people find themselves most at home on thresholds. Their
characteristic place in a church is the porch. They are 'boundary'
people, sometimes eccentric (because off-centre), often unpre-
dictable. But they may be the right ones to conduct rites of
passage, 'handing people over' from one mode of relationship
with the community to another while themselves remaining on
the threshold. They are not necessarily the community's leaders,
though they may become such if it is discerned that they also have
gifts of leadership (and those who are leaders will fulfil their
ministry best if they have some deep understanding of what it
means to be on the boundaries). Threshold people are valuable
precisely because they have come to be at home in the wilderness
and are able to guide others through a bewildering time of
transition, touching human lives at vulnerable moments, such as
birth, marriage, and death. The birth of a child marks not only

a transition from dependent to independent existence but also a recognition of new names for the adults – mother, father, grandparent. Various kinds of 'midwife' may be needed to 'attend' the birth. They are not 'one of the family' and they stand as a reminder of the break with the past, a symbol of dislocation as well as an encourager of the transition. They are therefore always at least slightly disturbing.

[Further, in a society which contains people of different faiths and many on the fringes of faith, which is often 'spiritual' in its perceptions of life having another dimension than that of the everyday but not always formally 'religious', we may expect to see a new kind of threshold person, one who is *not* identified with any one religious tradition. For example, in Australia there are now 'funeral celebrants' who know, both practically and spiritually, the territory of dying, death, and bereavement, and can help people find their own way, incorporating a variety of customs according to the faith and wishes of the mourners and of the one who has died.]

I should like to add a personal note. I find I have to guard against acting on feelings of unease, even of revulsion, when faced with 'evangelical dog collars' and 'catholic black suits'. I have to ask myself why I feel so strongly about this. One reason is that I am suspicious of religious certainties. A stronger reason is that these 'badges' symbolize for me, respectively, 'marriage' and 'celibacy' as the only permissible expressions of sexuality. If on the one hand you are gay or lesbian and on the other you are not drawn by God into the way of sexual solitude that is at the heart of celibacy, you are not going to be able to respond with complete honesty to the conditions which are part of the 'given' or 'ordained' ministry. You may feel called to the ministry of leadership, but in a peculiarly fundamental way you are unable to integrate your sexuality with it. You may then deny that sexuality or live it extremely privately, so existing in uneasy tension between expectation and reality. If you are a vicar you will regularly preside at the Eucharist, proclaiming that all creation and all human life is being offered to God for transformation, but not be able at any time to articulate and focus the offering of your sexuality, either on your own or on behalf of the substantial number of other human beings who share this particular aspect of humanity's variety. If you put an impenetrable wall around your sexuality and keep it totally private, your faith will become individualistic and your church will acquire the inward-looking character of the ghetto.

So you may find that you have to lay on one side the fulfilment of your vocation in the ministry of leadership. You search for another *place* for the living of your sexuality and your sense of vocation. Because you are already marginalized, you find that place on the margins, on the threshold. You have already experienced being society's small change, to be as nothing. So you can appreciate and contain the 'nothing', liminal, 'in-between' place, a place which by definition is without structure. The danger is that you can be so excluded as to fall permanently into that place of nothing and so belong nowhere at all. At best, however, your value in that place will be recognized. For it is a 'shamanic' place, you know both 'worlds', both 'before' and 'after' (partly out of a sense of yearning and exclusion), but you stay on the boundary, on the threshold. Otherwise there would be nobody waiting there to help those who wish to cross over. And it is a place where people have strange dreams – and you can help them to interpret the coded messages. You will be there at transition moments – birth, puberty, driving test, first job, graduation, marriage, partnership, divorce, retirement, serious operation, death. And you can help people look both to the past and to the future.

Without some such experience of being on the threshold for others, having no abiding city of your own, any ministry of leadership (if and when it becomes possible) will be simply one of conforming to the present. The celebration of repeated events like the Eucharist needs something of the subversive about it to prevent the self-satisfaction that comes from merely mirroring the values of the ecclesiastical or secular subculture in which you live.

Locating Ministries
in the Church

5

People with Particular Skills:
Contributing to the life of the Church

WHETHER by hidden presence, individual contribution, or publicly acknowledged apostleship, the ministries we have considered so far in this book have all been primarily 'located' in the world of personal relationships, work and community. All are called to be 'disciples', a few to be 'apostles'. By seeking to embody particular values and to be an embodied presence, by active engagement with everyday individual and corporate concerns, and by pioneering new forms of ministry in the midst of the secular, the People of God are already being a deaconing and priestly people. And we reached the point in the last chapter of seeing how a few of them also act in a representative way, recognized and commissioned to that kind of ministry by the Church. Often in small-scale and latent ways, they are exercising a role of pioneering leadership, 'going on before' to discover God, as always, already there ahead of them. They are exploring the new rather than sustaining the already established.

We now shift the perspective and ask how skills learned in the course of a person's education and working, personal, and community life can contribute to the ministries that need to be exercised within the corporate life of the Church itself, for its well-being, its worship and witness. Again we begin with the small-scale and humdrum, but noting that even when it is so easy to overlook what people give, all manner of contributions are continually being given for the common good and on behalf of the whole Christian community, and, indirectly, for the good of humankind and the whole creation. Such is the purpose of all the gifts of God. They are never given for the sole benefit of the recipient. They are not possessions or states of being but gifts to be shared. They are functions of 'service' through the 'energizing', the 'working', the 'operating' of the Holy Spirit. We shall see that while the gift of leadership shows this most clearly and publicly, yet it is also true of more modest ministries that are easily overlooked.

Moreover, we remember that Paul in 1 Corinthians 3.9 refers to God's 'fellow-workers' for the good of the whole creation. Our vision must be as wide as possible. 'Creation' is the priority, 'humanity' comes next, 'personal call' third, the 'variety of charisms' fourth, and the particular 'service' of leadership last. Would that it were and looked so!

The host of volunteers

There are numerous small-scale ministries undertaken voluntarily in local churches, each and every one necessary to the well-being of those churches – so that when a stranger visits she may recognize the features that make up the face of a genuine Christian community.

To these tasks some are appointed, some elected. Some join rotas, others take on a specific role for a few years. Some relate to occasional events, others are offices whose continuity spans centuries. Each draws on skills usually acquired elsewhere –

> in public speaking – lesson readers, intercessors;
> in 'theatre' – liturgists, stage managers etc;
> in music – organists, instrumentalists, choir leaders;
> in finance – treasurers, stewardship organisers;
> in administration – secretaries, sacristans,
>   churchwardens;
> in education – teachers;
> in befriending – pastoral carers.

Although experience in one church may recommend a person for similar ministry elsewhere, there is usually no principle involved which means that a person can expect a transfer – as there would be if there was a career structure. (There may be exceptions to this, as when organists, administrators, vergers, etc. work in a full-time and paid capacity in larger churches and cathedrals, simply because of the amount of work that needs to be done. But for the purposes of 'locating' ministries it may be useful to draw a distinction between what is voluntary and unpaid and what is professional and paid. More on the latter below.)

Some local churches have an annual service of 'dedication' and 'blessing', sometimes after the Annual General Meeting with its election of officers and committees. On such an occasion the whole community are given the opportunity of 'affirming' and 'recognizing' these ministries.

Skills acquired elsewhere may not completely equip a person to be competent in a new role. A certain amount of 'preparation' can be helpful. 'Training' is not the appropriate word, with its implications of qualifications and certificates, and with the feeling it may give that you can't be a Christian unless you've been through a series of tests. But there needs to be some method of passing on experience and of encouraging newcomers. Churchwardens, teachers of children, pastoral visitors and the like can all grow in confidence in this way.

In a large urban parish there may be sufficient resources to sustain a programme for that parish alone. In rural areas and in inner cities, groups of churches, preferably ecumenically, may come together to provide this kind of enabling preparation. The approach is that of encouragement and the building of confidence as hidden abilities are brought to light (or established abilities given new purpose and direction) and opportunities are given for them to be exercised.

'Roger' was persuaded by his new vicar to take part in a course that would give him confidence to use the pastoral gifts that others had already discerned in him. He said ruefully that the previous vicar had never disturbed the congregation at all. But Roger went on the course – twenty evenings once a week through the winter months. There wasn't much that he had to read and there were no essays to write. But he and the others on the course were encouraged to share their experiences and to reflect on them in the light of their Christian faith and an understanding of how human beings develop and relate to one another. It all made him think and gave him guidance as to how

to improve the pastoral care he was doing in the
parish. He didn't intend to be doing anything new
after the course ended, but he was looking forward to
being recognized by and being accountable to the
local church as a pastoral visitor. The vicar pointed
out that much medical care in China is given by
ordinary people with the minimum of preparation for
that work – a mix of first aid volunteer and trained
health visitor. They were called 'barefoot' doctors and
worked in local communities where they were
needed – in the fields and villages and towns rather
than in the hospitals and surgeries. In a similar way
here was a local church and its leader encouraging its
'barefoot' pastors.

Local groups of churches may thus build up teams of 'barefoot'
teachers, visitors, welcomers, and the like, those who minister
somewhere on the sprectrum between the informal and
occasional ways of friends and family and neighbours and the
formal and continuous ways of the full-time minister.

Again, a service of recognition, dedication, and blessing can
be helpful. A public occasion encourages mutual responsibility
and accountability and enables the 'barefoot' minister to act in
the name of the Church in that locality and not just as an
individual. And a service reminds us that all ministry is a gift of
God for which thanksgiving is our first and last response.

There is a parallel to this kind of ministry in the work of the
Samaritans. They are not full-time paid counsellors but part-
time voluntary befrienders who nevertheless have been prepared
well for their task and perform it as a member of an accountable
body. If, after some experience, they move to another part of the
country, they will recognized by another branch of the
Samaritans if they so wish.

One way of locating oneself on this spectrum of ministries is to
look at these indicators –

a.	from volunteer	*to*	professional;
b.	from occasional	*to*	continuous;
c.	from unpaid	*to*	fully paid;
d.	from short period of preparation	*to*	extending training;
e.	from part-time	*to*	full-time.

A lesson reader in church will score five out of five in the first column. A churchwarden will be almost the same, except that the office is continuous rather than occasional. Most barefoot visitors will also be in the first column.

Now look at some other ministries. For all of them there are appropriate beginning moments of recognition and affirmation, of dedication, of commissioning, and of blessing. But one of the skills already mentioned may be so specific in a particular person that it becomes distinctive of the character of his or her contribution in a full-time, fully trained, paid capacity. This is where some organists, vergers, and administrators locate their ministries, even if they do not seem to be valued in quite the same way as the ministry of leadership! More of that later in the book. But for now consider two other well-established ministries in the Church of England.

Readers

Readers find themselves in column 1 where *c* and *e* are concerned, in column 2 where *b* and *d* are concerned, and probably experience their ministry as somewhere in between where a. is concerned. They are trained in the conduct of worship and in preaching, and learn a considerable amount about the Bible and Doctrine. They may also learn about pastoral care and become part of the leadership team in a parish. This has come about in recent years because it has been argued that there needs to be some connection between the leadership of worship and the leadership of people. But if this is so, there seems little reason why they shouldn't become assistant vicars. Or is this an instance of the creeping power of the centre and the hidden assumption that vicars are the only real ministers?

Another kind of connection could be proposed. The ministry is of the Word. It is about preaching and communication. The very name 'reader' indicates that. The connection with people would then be made not in a pastoral direction but in a concern with how we use language, with public speaking, with literature, with storytelling. A ministry of the Word which is not interested in words for their own sake soon declines into pious cliché.

❖

Church Army Officers

Those who are commissioned as officers in the Church Army in the Church of England find themselves wholly in column 2 of the spectrum. They are trained to exercise the quite specific ministry of evangelism. But again, under the influence of the dominant pastoral model of ministry, that of the vicar, they are too easily thought to be 'second-class', an additional or substitute curate who does not even have the possibility of wider responsibility. But almost by default they may accrue to themselves some features of the ministry of leadership without being recognized as such. Would it not be better if they were quite clearly seen and deployed as evangelists, perhaps accountable not to the vicar of a parish but to the bishop of a diocese, and possibly part of an evangelistic team?

❖

We can think of other particular ministries which can for some people be all-engaging and thus characteristic and typical of their ministry besides those of evangelism and of communicating the Word. There is the teacher/educator/theologian; the healer/counsellor; the diocesan officer for social responsibility; the diocesan stewardship adviser. And so on.

Each ministry needs its moment of affirmation and recognition, of dedication, commissioning, and blessing. And could we not ask the same of organists, diocesan secretaries, vergers, and the like, rather than expect them simply to start a new job on a designated day? And should they not have the same pay structure? (Including lawyers?)

6

People who Lead:
Focusing, embodying, enabling, representing, serving communion

... people who are called to lead Christian communities, to work in and among the People of God in cells and small groups, geographically in neighbourhoods, parishes, and dioceses, and in associations and institutions.

The whole People of God are called to live in God's Love, and to minister in hidden, dispersed, and pioneering ways, in society and in the Church. Most of them are also called to exercise ministries of leadership, usually on a small scale and often for only a short time, among families and groups and for particular occasions. A few will be called to lead on a larger scale and for a longer time, so much so that this becomes their characteristic stance, their recognized place in the life of the community. The well-being, the good order, of the People of God needs them. They may be given titles like

> Representative Ministers – representative of God and of the People of God.

> 'Presbyteroi', 'Episcopoi' – more commonly Vicars, Rectors, Ministers, Presbyters, Parish Priests, Bishops.

> Servants of Communion.

We may think of each of the patterns of service described in the first chapters of this book as a sequence to be experienced and incarnated first, and only then included and enfolded into the ministry of leadership. We would not then extract the inexperienced out of the community and train them too early for a leadership that all too often has become detached from their and others' humanity. There is a wisdom in not allowing people to take on a ministry of leadership until they have reached the age of thirty. There should be no by-passing of *any* of the earlier stages.

Various images cluster round this role of leadership, many of them so powerful that in many people's minds 'vicars' or 'ministers' or 'parish priests' *are* the Church. Vicars may be dismissed with fondness by the English and treated as a humorous or sad irrelevance, and yet there are many who have been drawn to God through their ministry, through their simply having been around, in their person questioning fashionable -isms, in their words and deeds touching others in their hearts and minds. Those in their turn being drawn to exercise such a ministry are likely to have been influenced by one or more of them. And the local church needs someone to hold its life together, to keep the boundaries and fend off the fanatic and the one-sided, to make sure that it is Christian worship that is celebrated week by week and day by day, to enable the varied ministries of the people of that congregation, and to represent that community to the wider church and wider world.

Which of these words do you think illustrate the ministry of leadership and which obscure?

> Servant
> Lord
> Father
> Priest
> Steward
> Watchman
> Helmsman
> Captain
> Shepherd

> Guardian
> Ambassador
> Chairman
> President
> Orchestrator
> Producer

All but the last four words are directly biblical and nearly all lead us to visualize men. Is this a matter of divine truth or simply of historical circumstance and conditioning? Look at the list again and deliberately focus on women you know who would be described by each word. Ask too if there are other words to be added. Helper? Enabler? Animator? And this time think of men who could be so described.

Now ask which of these words describe what you would expect of such a leader? Is there anything that is exclusive to the leader or do you think others can do these tasks as well? And again do you more easily visualize men or women?

> Pray
> Preach
> Lead worship
> Care
> Counsel
> Evangelize
> Heal
> Teach
> Administer
> Reconcile
> Listen
> Inspire
> Enable
> Focus
> Embody
> Represent
> Guide

Any others? And is there any significance in our being able to visualize men more easily when we use nouns and women when we use verbs?

Hans Küng has pointed out that many of the functions we ascribe to leaders are not exclusive to them. But if leaders do not in practice concern themselves with them, either directly or indirectly, then nothing will happen. No one else has been given the gift/commission to make sure that certain things got done.[41]

If it is easy to slip into the way of thinking that the vicar *is* the church, we also need to remind ourselves of how varied are the patterns of the ministry of leadership, both ecumenically and within each denomination. There are fewer full-time leaders for small country parishes or congregations, and cities are so vast and anonymous that even when divided into parishes, the boundaries are artificial, the populations are large, and people are mobile. And over this century the number, for example, of full-time stipendiary clergy in the Church of England has declined from about 23,000 (1901) to 18,000 (1951) to 11,000 (1981). Much more could be said about the context of the ministry of leadership at the end of the century, but this is enough to show that we should not be surprised to see new patterns emerging in response to changed conditions. Here are four sketches of people exercising in one way or another this ministry.

'David', a curate, has fairly recently been ordained, having come through the well established system of university and theological college. He knows that many of his colleagues are talking about changing patterns of ministry, but he is content for the time being to be a curate (or apprentice vicar as one of his colleagues puts it), and he is looking forward to becoming a vicar himself in a few years' time. He can imagine no more marvellous job. He is just discovering what a great privilege it is to preach and to preside at Holy Communion, and to be able to spend time freely with all kinds of people. And he does believe it is right to give firm leadership and to proclaim the Gospel as the answer to people's deepest needs. He doesn't know whether he'll be at his best as one of a team: he does have a desire to run his own show. He knows there are dangers in this – empire-building and all that – but he doesn't see how you can avoid there being a hierarchy of authority, with one person at the top. He does believe that exercising the responsibility (the buck does stop here, under God) goes along with the power to make decisions.

'Brenda' is a house group leader on a dead-end estate almost hemmed in by two trunk roads. There is only one way in and out. She has lived there for fifteen years – ever since her husband Jack got a job as a welder at the works down by the railway. They are the only family from the estate that goes to the parish church – a lovely building, but it's a mile and a half away, and it's not easy to get there a lot of the time. They have three children of school age and Jack's mother lives with them as well. But Brenda has been helping to bring the local church to the estate. The church council suggested that the parish needed house groups in the various estates and neighbourhoods. This would give people a chance to meet when they find it hard to get to church because of the distance or the weather or shift work. She was surprised when the vicar asked her to lead a group on the estate. She told him he was scraping the barrel, only to get the reply that there wasn't anyone else in the barrel! But it's made her think how to talk about her faith to her neighbours. She has the honesty to admit that she doesn't find sermons in church much help. For her it's simply the story of Jesus that she can't get away from.

So the group started by telling each other stories –
and then finding that the story of Jesus and their own
stories weren't all that far apart . . .

'John', a non-stipendiary minister, is a dentist by
profession and works in a busy market town. He and
his colleagues have so arranged the group practice
that he can go in four days a week. He has to admit
that he easily earns more than enough to survive. He
and his wife have paid off nearly all the mortgage on
their house now, helped by a recent inheritance from
his father. For the last ten years they've been living in
a village about six miles out of town. About five years
ago, their vicar finally retired. He was over eighty –
old enough for the rules about retirement to have
passed him by! Theirs is a small village and they knew
there wasn't a chance of having another full-time
vicar. Nor frankly would it have made sense with a
population of only two hundred. But no one wanted to
see the church disappear and they weren't too keen on
sharing a vicar with six other small parishes and so
seeing him for a breathless hour or less on a Sunday
morning. But they regularly have a congregation of
twenty or thirty and on the folk occasions nearly half
the village turns out. John had been feeling the
pressure of a call to minister for some time, but he'd
never been able to see a way forward without having
to give up dentistry – and it never seemed right to do
that. Then the opportunity came to do a course of
training in the evenings and at weekends, and he was
ordained three years ago. He is usually available on
Sundays and on one other day of the week, and that's
all that's needed to co-ordinate the life and work of the
church in the village. Inevitably it's on a small scale,
and other people do more than they ever did in the old
days. But they always seem to cope together, even
when there's an emergency. He is sure full-timers will
always be needed, but he thinks it would be better if

they worked in the market town and in two of the
larger villages, with perhaps the Rural Dean co-
ordinating the ministries of a dozen or more like him.
They might also have particular gifts among them to
share with all the churches of the area – youth work or
adult education or whatever. He is also sure they need
to know they're part of a church that is much bigger
than their own small locality. That's why they
appreciate seeing the bishop from time to time,
representing as he does the wider church and
guarding and guiding the local ones. They don't want
to become a village sect!

'Susan' reminisces about the time she was a parish
worker. For many years she had been a social worker,
and had spent a good deal of time with troubled
adolescents. She had taken care to keep abreast of new
methods of training in pastoral care and counselling:
for some years she had taught these skills to
theological students. But times were changing and she
was looking for a new direction. She lived on the edge
of town in a bungalow which she valued very much as
'home' and worshipped at the local church down the
road. It was not much of a place to look at – it had
been the daughter church of a parish for many years.
But somehow the building was in Susan's bones.
About the time she was wondering what to do next,
the priest-in-charge of the parish moved, and there
didn't seem to be much chance of a successor. Out of
the blue she was asked if she would look after the
parish. Now she had never thought of being ordained,
but she couldn't think of any good reason to say 'No' to
this request – though she tried hard! Everyone in the
parish thought it was a good idea, and the bishop was
keen. And she enjoyed the five years she spent leading
that small community. It did seem rather strange to
have the local hospital chaplain coming in for an hour
on a Sunday morning to preside at the Eucharist.

His pastoral responsibilities were elsewhere and
he didn't have time to belong in the parish. He didn't
live far away but he couldn't be involved in the life of
the people in the way Susan was free to be. There was
no particular tension between them. It just felt odd,
that's all...

How might those experiences be included in our understanding
of this ministry of leadership? Historically, there is no clear
answer. Indeed, in the early years of the Church, though the
need for leadership was perceived as vital, it was fulfilled in a
variety of ways, in the spirit of service, for the building up of the
Body and for its mission. But there was no blueprint. There were
ministries, there was leadership. Beyond that, there is nothing
we can say with certainty. If there was a succession of leaders, it
was not mechanical as if by acts of magic, nor was it by virtue of
a settled and recognized office over and distinct from the rest of
the Church. 'Apostolic succession' was transmitted by the loyalty
of the whole Christian community to the Gospel of Jesus Christ,
even if it was found appropriate to focus the responsibility for
keeping the community loyal on 'servants of communion' set
apart for that ministry.

'Priest' and 'apostle' are not central to the description of the
Christian in the New Testament. We read of the sacrificial
quality of the being and living of the believer, but 'priest' is used
as an image of this, not as a definition. And 'being sent' is
understood to be part of the movement of God interpenetrating
the world, but such 'apostleship' is again only an image of this
fundamental mission. And let us recall that if there is a basic
word to describe the Christian it is 'disciple', the one who is
responding to the invitation of Jesus to 'follow me'.

Now if the particular significance of the Apostles is their
unique witness to the Resurrection (which includes some
women), and they passed on this witness to Resurrection Life,
then it is the following together in word and deed in the Way of
the Risen Christ that constitutes 'apostolic succession'. Within
these communities a few may be called to focus this life in the
ministry of leadership, but they are not the source of the life

of the community. Only the Spirit of the Risen Christ can be that.

Leadership, like any other ministry, is a *gift,* a *charism,* always to be exercised as a *service,* a *diakonia.* All such gifts are given for the purpose of building up the whole Body, for *koinonia,* for fellowship, community, communion.

In time, new words come to be used to describe such leaders, words taken from the everyday language of the city council. 'Presbuteroi' and 'episcopoi' are 'elders' and 'overseers', with the role of the episcopoi being that of chairmen.

Now according to what one is already inclined to believe, the temptation is either to emphasize the chaos and variety of the early days and to play down any move towards order and continuity, or to discern and stress those indications of a settling down to a permanent pattern, fixed for all time. In any case, throughout the history of the Church there has been a tension between order and variety, continuity and innovation.

By paying attention to that history and to the movements and pressures of our own time, we may be able to identify for this ministry of leadership certain characteristic features as well as certain variables.

Characteristic features

1. 'Servants of communion' are co-ordinators of the ministries of the People of God, those who enable and inspire others to fulfil their particular ministries of caring, evangelizing, teaching, healing etc. It is a task of consolidation, of edification, of building up the community. In the best sense of the word it is a ministry of administration and organisation, avoiding the temptations of the authoritarian, the bureaucratic, and the patriarchal, and alert to 'servanthood'.

2. 'Servants of communion' are most typically and symbolically so when they preside at the Eucharist, 'administering' Holy Communion. They preside at the Ministry of the Word, they are Guardians of that Word, responsible for the preaching if not necessarily engaged in it on every occasion. To do this they need to listen prayerfully to people and to God, to seek to

relate the major questions of life to faith in Christ, and to articulate the will of God for the community. They preside too at the Ministry of the Sacrament, they are Guardians of that Sacrament, responsible for enabling the community to remember Christ with thanksgiving and to be united in sharing the Sacrament of Christ's Living Presence. They make clear in a focused way what is *already* present in a diffused way.

3. 'Servants of communion' are called to focus and embody the unity and continuity of the People of God. Witness those lists of vicars at the back of churches and of bishops in cathedrals. In Catholic tradition this means that no local church can by itself be the source of its own leader: there must be reference in some way to the wider body. Protestant traditions place more emphasis on the sufficiency of each local congregation as the Church. Certain tasks of leadership are delegated to the Minister, who thus bears this ministry independently of other local churches. In this understanding the unity and continuity is in spirit and in loyalty to faith in Jesus Christ.

> "In order to fulfil its mission, the Church needs persons who are publicly and continually responsible for pointing to its fundamental dependence on Jesus Christ, and thereby provide, within a multiplicity of gifts, a focus for its unity. The ministry of such persons, who since very early times have been ordained, is constitutive for the life and witness of the Church."[42]

4. 'Servants of communion' are called to guard the faith we have all inherited and to oversee the community that is called to embody that faith.

5. 'Servants of communion' are given their ministry by God, authorized by God, and empowered by the Spirit of God. The People of God assembled must give their assent to one newly appointed and also delegate the ministry which is corporately embodied in them all.

❖

Variable features

1. The ministry of leadership does not have to be a one-man band. It may be exercised corporately, on a collegiate model, e.g. diocesan and area bishops; team rector and vicars.

2. It does not have to be full-time.

3. It does not have to be for life. Such ministers may become incognito again or take on a pioneering ministry. And they will probably retire.

4. They do not have to be paid a stipend. They may be paid in part or not at all, having retired early from other work on an adequate pension. [So in terms of the spectrum outlined in the previous chapter, such ministers are likely to be between the two columns where *a, b,* and *d* are concerned, but may be in the first where *c* and *e* are concerned.]

5. They do not have to live in houses that proclaim a higher social status than those among whom they live. Ordinary houses in village streets have sufficed in the past. Bungalows and belfries are not unknown.

6. Some would not think they have to be either celibate or male or both. The removal of that restriction can at least be reasonably argued, and in some churches it is now common practice.

7. They do not have to wear academic hoods on their backs. University degrees are hardly essential even if intelligence is.

It might be helpful to refer to some sociological thinking about associations of human beings.[43] A distinction can be drawn between primary groups, communities, and societies. A 'primary group' is the cell, family or household, with small numbers and intimate relationships. A 'community' is an association characterized by shared values and commitments which are orientated round a significant aspect of human life, with plenty of personal exchange in a spirit of mutuality and interdependence. Such can be a local church, or, in the words of the liberation theologian, Leonardo Boff, a 'base community' – consisting, he thinks, of some fifteen to twenty primary groups. Such a church can have a sense of gathering in one place in the name of Christ for regular participation in the Word and Sacrament. A 'society', however, is a more formal organization that is structured round office holders who are recognized as the competent authority and where there are explicit rules to be adhered to. Is the challenge to the Church to become a 'communion of communities' rather than a society? Office holders are doubtless necessary, but is their vision one of an institution or of a living organism? Is the hard task of those in office to encourage the flourishing of the values of the living communities? Has not the thinking of the largest scale, the provincial, national, and worldwide come to spread over and dominate the life of the local? We do not often see the principle of subsidiarity in practice.

First, then, a description of what is usually the case. Because the Church is so often equated with churches, and because of the division of responsibility by geographical area, the ministry of leadership is inevitably dominated by those who are given the pastoral charge of such recognizable pieces of territory. The scale of course varies:

> the local parish whether a village or housing estate with one person in charge, perhaps part-time and non-stipendiary, or a town or part of a city, with a full-time vicar and possibly assistants;

> a group of parishes often known as a deanery or a circuit, with a rural dean or a superintendent minister exercising pastoral oversight;

> a larger area: a diocese with its bishop, a district with its chairman;

> and a larger area still: a province with its archbishop;

> and on the world scale: for Roman Catholics the Pope (one of whose titles is 'servant of the servants of God'), for Anglicans the Archbishop of Canterbury who has a primacy of honour but not of jurisdiction.

The area of responsibility may be more narrowly defined, but still have a geographical location. There are chaplains to colleges, ships, factories, prisons, hospitals, regiments, parliaments, and other institutions.

Less easy to grasp are the ministries of leadership exercised across geographical boundaries, often where people gather not in special buildings but for special occasions. Here is a ministry among mobile communities, among associations or networks, among actors, among minority groups or people at leisure.

Most of us who live in cities and towns are dispersed through many different communities and networks. We may belong to several. This is particularly true in active adult life. So we find a tendency for local churches to attract those whose lives are more domestic, more home-based, least mobile – the very young, the very old, and the ill, those who have not yet entered, or who have retired from, or have temporarily withdrawn from, the mainstream of the life of our society, with all its complexity, decision-making, changes, and growth. There is the danger of the Church being privatized in its concerns and retreating from engagement with the secular world. The need is for alertness and action to increase the presence of pioneers in new places and to expect as a result of their mission new forms of 'church', of worship and fellowship.

The ministry of leadership arises out of and in the midst of a network of relationships in the Christian community. Representative ministry and the community represented are inseparable. Ministers may represent the community to the wider world and may represent the wider Church to the local church, but they are not set either above or over against the community.

> "All members of the believing community, ordained and lay, are interrelated. On the one hand, the community needs ordained ministers. Their presence reminds the community of the divine initiative, and of the dependence of the Church on Jesus Christ, who is the source of its mission and the foundation of its unity. They serve to build up the community in Christ

and to strengthen its witness. In them the Church
seeks an example of holiness and loving concern. On
the other hand, the ordained ministry has no
existence apart from the community. They cannot
dispense with the recognition, the support, and the
encouragement of the community."[44]

Power based on exclusive claims and used to dominate and
subdue has no place in Christian leadership, whether this be to
seek status in the sanctuary or to claim to be speaking the
definitive word of God by direct inspiration. Someone said that
if all power corrupts and absolute power corrupts absolutely,
ecclesiastical power corrupts diabolically.

Rather does leadership arise out of a gift for making and
sustaining relationships with people. Presiding at the Eucharist
is an appropriate and significant – some would argue *the* most
appropriate and significant – public expression of the
leadership, that service of communion. It is the People of God
who celebrate the Eucharist and need good leadership to enable
that to happen rather than the leader holding a unique power,
sealed off from the people and handed down exclusively from one
generation to the next. It is more a matter of 'without leadership
the Body cannot thrive' rather than 'without leadership the
Eucharist cannot happen'.[45]

❖

Some questions:

1. If the People of God celebrate the Eucharist and if continuing
   leadership of a particular community has not yet evolved, is it
   appropriate, if possibly irregular, for the group to designate
   one of its number to preside, albeit temporarily? How do you
   see the relationship between community, leader and
   Eucharist?

2. If leadership of an organisation or association is invested in an
   elected committe, one of whose tasks is to nurture the network
   of relationships that comprises the membership, and if the
   organisation wishes from time to time to focus its life in
   worship, then who takes the decisions as to the form of that
   worship and who takes the leading parts in its conduct?

3. Is the role of presiding at the Eucharist more like that of the producer of a play or like that of the leading actor? Are there valid reasons for the President alone saying the Prayer of Thanksgiving over the bread and wine rather than the whole assembly? Historically, the best analogy may be that of the head of the Jewish household who 'said grace' at domestic prayer. Does the analogy hold? And is the one who breaks bread the host or the waiter? And who serves? And in what order do people feed?

4. Is too much fuss made of ordinations and inductions as at present conducted, with the visual message that bishops and vicars are the most important people in the Church and that these are the most significant occasions of Christian commitment? Should the emphasis be rather on baptism and confirmation? If too much power and responsibility is given to one person, how can one convey the reality of servanthood rather than lordship?

5. If you feel drawn to this role of presiding at the Eucharist, what are your motives? Visible status? Ego-boosting costume? Exclusive powers of consecration? Unconsecrated actor? Seeking status because you are unconvinced that you have value and worth in yourself? Further, does this desire connect with gifts of pastoral relationships and leadership? Are you able to draw close to others and remain close to them? Do you – perhaps only half-consciously – perceive this ministry as a retreat from secular complexities? Is it not rather a challenge to enter more deeply into every part of life?

6. Some sense their call from God as direct to them as individuals. They talk easily of the living and accessible presence of Jesus and of the indwelling of the Holy Spirit. Others sense their call from God as the Church (through one or more of its members) suggesting that they have the potential to exercise pastoral leadership, serving the unity and communion of the Church. The first group need to beware of being subjective, even fanatical in self-confidence, and remember that all gifts of the Spirit are for the sake of the building up of the Body. The First Letter of John warns us

that mere reference to the gift of the Spirit is not enough to keep a community true to the Gospel. The second group need to ask if ambition for institutional power is not lurking as a hidden motive. To which group do you belong?

7. Throughout this chapter the assumption has been made that there is little distinction *in principle* between vicars and bishops. So what do you make of these sets of statements?

   a. The only difference between them is the scale of their responsibility; *or*

   There is a difference in principle, in kind, as well as in responsibility;

   Bishops, who have the task of guardianship and overseeing, delegate these tasks when needed to local vicars, but only bishops are really necessary; *or*

   A vicar is not the representative of the bishop but directly and independently a bearer of the ministry of leadership.

   b. There is no *necessary* link between local churches; *or*

   The local church is a manifestation of, not a branch of the universal Church; *or*

   The bishop represents and enables the universality of the Church.

   c. The historic threefold ministry of bishops, priests, and deacons is of the very *being* of the Church; *or*

   No, but it is for the Church's *well-being*; *or*

   Rather, it is for the Church's 'fulness of being'; *or*

   There is really only *one* order of the ministry of leadership, with different scales of responsibility; *or*

   There is only *one sacrament* of ordination, though it looks as if there are three. The Book of Common Prayer talks of the making of deacons, the ordination of priests, and the consecration of bishops. If makings and consecrations are not ordinations, what are they?

CURRENT EXAMPLE 1: *'Local' 'ordained' ministers — presbyters of small parishes.*

Here is an example of those ministers who are (see p. 53) in column 1 where *c* and *e* are concerned and between the columns where *a*, *b*, and *d* are concerned, upaid and part-time, but ministering over a period of years, not simply in a voluntary capacity, and having been trained.

The pressure towards this kind of ministry has come from depopulated rural areas in this country. It can in some ways be paralleled with the situation in parts of Africa and Latin America where 'base communities' have grown up and where questions are being asked about whether a full-time 'priest' ministering to a number of scattered communities and seeing each one only once a year is an appropriate pattern of leadership.

The idea is that a person who has begun to show gifts of leadership in his or her local church should receive some training and that those trained gifts should be recognized in the ordination of that person, but that the licence to minister should be restricted quite clearly to the place where he or she already lives.

This is a pattern of leadership which emerges from 'below' and is bound to disturb the pattern which is given from 'above'. A 'local' minister restricted to one place is different from the minister who in principle can move anywhere in the Church, from place to place over a working lifetime. Perhaps we should affirm that principle while recognizing that in practice a change of place will depend upon abilities and experience and circumstances (as is current practice when appointing vicars to parishes with unusual needs and when distinguishing between the qualities needed to lead a cathedral community – as Dean – and those needed to preside over the life of a diocese – as Bishop.) And there will be some leaders who are indeed content to exercise their ministry on a small scale in one locality for a number of years, not least because another commitment (perhaps as a farmer) keeps them committed to that specific parish.

As regards training, the model may well be that of the apprentice who is alongside one more experienced. Courses are devised which do not involve a person moving house and attending a residential college, but are run in evenings and at weekends in a centre within reasonable distance from home. Such a course will not be academic, but will equip a person with skills of reflection, listening, speaking, and thinking that will give them access not only to the resources of Christian faith and worship, but also to the lives of those with whom they will have to do as leaders of Christian communities.

Roland Allen wrote in 1912 that in an illiterate (i.e. unacademic and visual) society "a holy illiterate, if gifted with common sense and the respect of his fellows, would make not only a suitable but the *right* leader for an illiterate church."[46] Even if society today is not illiterate, the Church is often far too literate for people who are not academic and who learn visually more easily than verbally. Professionals with words can, often without realizing it, oppress the inarticulate.

Of course there is a danger in all this that a local church with its local minister can become an isolated congregation independent of the rest of the worldwide Church and in danger of becoming sectarian and odd. For those with any sense of catholicity, however small the 'c', it is important to be reminded that they are more than a local congregation, not simply a private club choosing its leader from an inner core of activists. Moreover, villages and inner cities contain a mixture of people who easily cross over parish boundaries: local communities are not all that 'local' any more, in the sense of being static and self-contained. And sometimes an 'outsider' is not identified with this or that section of the local community and may be more effective in bringing together the different parts of that community.

Change the angle of vision a little and we might see a pattern of ministry whereby leadership is exercised both by one of the natural leaders in the locality and by those who on the one hand bring in particular skills from outside from time to time, and on the other hand offer encouragement and guidance from a perspective gained from oversight over a number of communities.

An interesting perspective is given by Vincent Donovan who 'pitched his tent' as a missionary among the Masai of Africa. He is a Roman Catholic priest and for a while he celebrated the

Eucharist on his own, in secret in his tent. He then came to realize that this was inappropriate. The celebration of the Eucharist did not make sense without a community of people. He began to long for the first Baptisms. Then, to his dismay, he realized that he would never preside at the Eucharist there because he was not, nor ever could be, the leader of a community of the Masai. He might on some future occasion be invited to preside as a representative of the wider church, but he could not be designated as the presbyter of that local church. That had to be the person who was able to call and hold together that particular body of people. He had to recognize that the ministry of the missionary was different from that of the presbyter. He had thought otherwise only because his own culture had lost the sense of a given community, of being *vitally* in relation to one another. In a Masai village there were *already* those who would emerge as preacher, prophet, teacher, singer, presbyter.[47]

CURRENT EXAMPLE 2: *'Non-stipendiary' and 'professional' ministers*

There are overlaps in this example with the previous one, in that another new category of the ministry of leadership has grown up alongside the well-established full-time professional vicar. This has raised the uncomfortable question as to whether or not you can be a leader in the Church without being a member of a professional clerical élite or caste. In his book *The Clerical Profession,* Anthony Russell has explored the historical background to this as well as the contemporary tensions within the Church of England.[48]

In the eighteenth century some clergy were also politicians, Poor Law administrators, land tax commissioners, local government officials, social welfare officers, teachers and magistrates. During the following century this range of functions contracted, as it did in other walks of life, e.g. lawyers no longer engaged in the management of estates. Also the actual functions of the clergy grew more and more specific, in fact largely liturgical and pastoral. Also appropriate knowledge and skills were acquired, including a professional language, again paralleled in specialized competence in other professions, with professional journals and conferences.

This has had the effect of setting the clergy apart from the dominant culture, often bolstered theologically by an understanding of holiness that emphasizes apartness. Rectories developed their own sub-culture, distinctive clerical dress was re-adopted, clerical mannerisms and voice became more common as clergy became less at ease with people, and a rudimentary career structure appeared, along with the founding of theological colleges. The hallmark of the Church of England was to be a "learned clerk and gentleman" in every parish. So clergy came from a narrow social and academic band, linked by family and education with those in power.

Increasingly, however, as society became more urban and complex and secular while the structures of the Church remained paternalist and hierarchical, church-going became an optional leisure activity that had to compete with others on offer. Bishops opposed Sunday newspapers and bicycling clubs and clergy became "the bearers of a traditional home-centred culture" focused on women, children, and leisure rather than on pubs, sport, and work. By the end of the First World War, during which army chaplains were not allowed to go to the front line, the Church had been identified with the clergy and that implied being out of touch.

In other ways, too, clergy were becoming marginalized. Even their pastoral and liturgical functions were delegated (or simply done by others anyway – social workers, citizens' advice bureaux, Samaritans). Preaching became a minor influence on people's lives compared with other means of communication. Even as a representative figure, the vicar no longer represented the wider community, only the Christian community. Life was becoming increasingly privatized.

Yet the picture of the Church as the Vicar remained. Even an increase in corporate styles of leadership, in teams and groups, has not changed the picture greatly and has brought its own tensions, not least when tensions between women and men have been added to those between corporate and singular styles. Any ministries among paid professional clergy that have gone beyond the familiar parishes, hospitals, schools, prisons, and the forces have been very much in a minority. In a society orientated towards work in large complex organisations (in most cities the three major employers are the local council, the health service, and education), clergy are perceived as 'non-work' and have contact with most people only at occasional rituals.

The growth of non-stipendiary ministry has to be seen against this background, perceived by the professionals as a sub-profession and only gradually being recognized as a challenge to re-interpret ministry as such. The growth has happened for at least three reasons, all connected with what has been happening with the professionals:

a. A decline in the number of full-timers.
b. A decline in the proportion of endowment income in the payment of the clergy.
c. The success of the Liturgical Movement, with the Eucharist much more at the centre of the Church's worship than in the past.

So far, however, most of those in non-stipendiary ministry are members of other professions! Unlike the first example, they do not necessarily emerge from the pressure of local needs, where the church is geographically isolated or numerically weak. And both 'professional' and 'non-stipendiary' rarely inhabit the language and thought forms of working class culture. Not much has been done to counteract the defensiveness of the professionals against power and responsibility being claimed by 'lay' people. The models of leadership are still drawn from the armed services and older form of hierarchical industrial management rather than from newer models in industry or from voluntary associations with their minimum of paid professionals and maximum of local unpaid leadership that encourages participation by as many members as possible.

So Anthony Russell. And more personally –

> 'Stephanie' is leaving her parish. The last straw was the organ appeal. The church council decided to go ahead with raising £20,000. And as the deacon in charge she was supposed to be giving a lead and taking up fund-raising with enthusiasm. She couldn't do it.

It went against her deepest convictions about the Church being for people and their needs. And she was convinced they didn't need a big triumphalist musical instrument to lead their singing in worship. There didn't seem to be any concern for the thousands of people in the parish who never came near the church. Most of the congregation in fact came from the small pockets of private housing scattered among the various large council estates. She recalled how she had been shocked on the night of her licensing to hear that it clashed with the community centre's reception for local councillors. And there was another thing. No one wanted to take any responsibility in the Church. Not that she was wanting to abdicate leadership. Far from it. But she didn't think of herself as on a pedestal – more as part of the community, not above it. She wanted to serve people, but so often she felt they lived in entirely different worlds. The Church seemed so inward-looking it made her despair. And what next for her? As yet she doesn't know. She still wants to minister in some way but doesn't think she will see the way ahead clearly for quite a while yet.

Reshaping Ministries

7
People with Power:
Exercising an unusual kind of authority

As soon as we begin to reflect on matters of ministry and leadership we come up against issues of authority. Looked at in one way there is no problem: it is God who calls, initiates, authorizes; the People of God call and authorize one of their number to a particular ministry only in God's name. At an ordination service the emphasis is on the gift of *God* through prayer and the laying on of hands. There are also gifts of the Spirit which a person may unexpectedly receive and which others later recognize as carrying their own intrinsic authority. But none of these affirmations answers all the questions about the nature and purpose of such God-given authority, nor about how it should be exercised.

To begin with, human beings work with different models of authority in different circumstances. We are all most familiar with the pyramid. There may be the Minister, the Elders, and the People of a Presbyterian Church, or the Bishop, Vicars, and People of an Anglican Diocese. Even the most fiercely independent of local congregations have this kind of structure. It is never long before a collection of individuals realizes that individualism run riot leads to chaos not harmony. But do we too easily adopt without question the most familiar patterns of authority from the surrounding culture?

Of course there is a strong argument that says that human beings are hierarchical animals, that this structure is biologically inbuilt, and that it cannot be changed, only used in more or less humane ways. The psychiatrist David Stafford-Clark claimed that we can never be free of this inherited dependence because a hierarchy is just as characteristic of our nervous systems as of those of any other social animal.[49]

79

Some questions:

1. *Is* biology destiny? Is a hierarchical model the only one? Certainly it sits easily with certain 'masculine' traits of character, with an emphasis on coercive power, and with the desire for the exercise of that power, often at the expense of those below. It is interesting that the Church has often allied itself to monarchies and dictatorships – and mirrored them in its own organisation. Metaphors of leadership are often drawn from military models. The Pope has been likened to an admiral on the flagship of a fleet. Now is it the case that the military is the source of the metaphor or that these pyramidal structures simply parallel one another, all of them reflecting a fundamental biological structure? And is that the last word from biology?

2. Hierarchies usually imply passive, obedient people who have no real responsibilities for participating in making decisions, only in carrying them out. The story is told of a new vicar who arrived at the church for Evensong on his first Sunday. It was dark and he stumbled around for a while until he located the light switches. To his astonishment there were a number of people already sitting in the pews. Asked why nobody had turned on the lights, one man replied, "The Vicar always does that."

3. Add to the hierarchical structure the increased separation of the clergy during the past century, not least through theological training and qualification, and we are almost bound to live with a division between 'them' and 'us'. The 'professionals' have, like enclosure landlords, taken to themselves more and more 'expert' theological, liturgical and pastoral knowledge excluding the 'laity' from their common land.

4. How much do adults slip into the role of children and pupils in church, looking to father figures for security and teachers for answers? Is this caricature or reality? Does the way we order our common life encourage people to grow into maturity in Christ? What do the arrangement of furnishings

in churches actually communicate about our corporate life? The Gothic echoes the imperial court with the emperor on a dais, and the Protestant echoes the law court and the schoolroom with the Minister as judge and teacher.

5. If the Christian presbyter is modelled on the kind of priest-figure of many ancient and not so ancient societies, care must be taken for it *not* to be about power exercised *over* people, a power to do exclusive things, membership of a privileged caste. In Christ the location of the holy has become the everyday.

In the Graeco-Roman and Jewish world with its authoritarian, patriarchal and hierarchical understanding of leadership, and its notions of priesthood, it was inevitable that Christian ministry took the shape it did over the first two or three centuries. There were no other structures through which the Christian Gospel could find corporate expression. But it may not be the only, nor the best, way of embedding in our life together the service of friendship in Christ to which we are called.

It is interesting that Vincent Donovan discovered that the word chosen by the people of the Masai village for their leader in Christ was not that for chief or powerful one or witch doctor or head or even shepherd, but 'ilaretok' – helper or servant of the community, one who was *already* there among them.[50]

Change the pyramid to a cone and flatten it, and you have the model of concentric circles, the hierarchy with a human face, less of rule and more of service, with movement into and out of the centre rather than up to the top and down to the bottom. Consistent with this model is talk of spheres of responsibility and the need to have somebody – or a few people – at the centre to serve and hold together the whole.

However, the centre may still hold all the power. There is no necessary change of structure, only a way of thinking about it and possibly a way of operating it. Certainly the practice of the Church of England has moved towards this model over the past generation. Bishops are less keen to be addressed as 'My Lord', and some vicars are more modest in the limelight. An open letter to the papal conclave of 1978 asked for a Pope who would be "judicious and sensible in the manner of contemporary leadership, exercising his authority not by issuing decrees but by giving reasons, not by making lonely decisions in isolation, but by wrestling for common consensus in open dialogue..."

Even where this shift is taking place there is still an authoritarian tail that can sting. The talk – and some of the practice – may indeed by of 'service' and even of 'friendship', but when the spirit of co-operation fails, confrontation tends still to be conducted in the style of the pyramid. The shock can be nastier for its being less expected.

Further, if there is pressure for even greater change because of debates and desires for new understandings of faith and practice, the inherited model, in either 'conservative' or 'liberal' form will feel more and more inflexible, unable to meet new and complex demands. The response is either to operate the pyramid more rigidly or to explore new possibilities altogether.

So to a third model – that of 'systems'. In chapter 9 of his book *The Turning Point*, Fritzjof Capra[51] discusses the characteristics of living organisms under the heading, 'The Systems View of Life'. This might be a helpful model for those who understand their organisation as a living organism, a Body. Biology might even be destiny – but not perhaps as we have pictured biology so far.

In this perspective, each organism is a self-organising system whose shape and size is established according to its own inner dynamic. At the same time it is an open system, porous to its environment, with which it interacts continually. Each organism maintains its overall structure in spite of change and the replacement of its component parts – each of which in turn is a self-organising system. A cell continues to look the same, even though this could not be predicted from simply observing the constant change of molecules, organelles and macromolecules. So in one sense the whole is contained within each of the parts and in another sense the whole is something other than the sum of these individual parts.

The whole biosphere is a dynamic, complex, interrelated, and integrated web of living and non-living forms. It is 'multi-levelled', though 'level' is a term for the place from which the observer observes, used for analysis and convenience only. For there are transactions and inter-dependencies among and between all the levels. Organisms tend to associate, establish links, live inside one another, and co-operate. Indeed, any competition takes place within the larger context of co-operation.

Capra illustrates this with a 'tree-diagram', from the cells as 'fronds', though the tissues, organ, and organ system, to the 'trunk', the organism itself. He comments that 'hierarchy' is an unsuitable word in this context because there are *many* intricate and non-linear pathways along which signals of information and transaction travel between all levels, 'ascending' and 'descending'. Power is exercised in *both* directions, neither dominating. And the purpose of the points of exchange is not for control but for the most helpful way of organising the complexity.

It is not hard to think of illustrations of the way in which our complex lives today push us in the direction of some such model as this, with authority dispersed, moving from one person to another and from one group to another in different and often rapidly changing circumstances, such authority being understood and practised less in terms of title and status and office and more in terms of function and knowledge and trustworthiness and quality of service.

Here are some samples from contemporary life to illustrate how in fact we are increasingly organizing our lives according to this third model:

Five hundred years ago, it would have been reasonable to claim to have read every book that had been written. Today nobody can remotely make that claim. Any leader depends on the selecting and culling of information from many sources, written and oral. Each contribution will have its own degree of authority. Consequently, leaders working for the good of the whole are bound to experience that oversight in a corporate and somewhat diffused way.

Are committees chaired by a permanently designated office-
holder, or does the role circulate among those members who are
competent to chair meetings? We experience a tension between
these two models.

An engineer had the task of drawing up a plan of roles and
relationships for an eighteen-month project being undertaken by
two hundred people. So complex were the interactions and
shifting patterns that he said he need at least four dimensions for
an adequate illustrative model.

With decreasing emphasis on paid full-time employment for life
in one field of work, more and more people are hesitant about
being known definitively by their position. Rather than say, "I
am a teacher," a person may be more comfortable with, "I used
to teach but now I'm helping to monitor climatic change with a
meteorological agency." Or, "I teach part-time these days; I also
write articles, I play with my grandchildren, I work an
allotment, I drive a van for Meals-on-Wheels." We still use
nouns like 'teacher' or 'vicar' or 'stonemason', with the
implication of 'what I do is derived from who I am.' But this is in
tension with an increasing use of verbs, with the implication of
'who I am is derived from what I do and how I relate.' Here is a
shift of perception, not to be accepted uncritically, but to be
acknowledged and lived with. Even if we still use the nouns, we
have to recognize that there are many ways now of being a
'teacher' or a 'minister', and many new descriptions within any
one field of work – hundreds, for example, in a large hospital.

A church at Ronchamp in eastern France was so designed by Le
Corbusier as to have, apart from its vertical walls, no straight
lines. Floor and ceiling slope in waves, walls curve in and out, a
circular chapel is discovered unexpectedly round a corner, lit by
a shaft of light from a stained-glass window far above. Nearly

everything is in movement: the eye comes to a temporary halt only at the altar. Le Corbusier said that in designing the church he had in mind a symbol of our own century: radio transmitters and receivers which point to the living processes of movement and communication and relationships.

The status symbol of a successful American business has been the sleek skyscraper housing the head office, a kind of secular Vatican or, more modestly, Lambeth. Because of the revolution in the storage and exchange of information, such buildings are becoming redundant. The leadership team of a large international corporation begins to resemble a travelling university faculty. Fewer personnel stay in one role in one place for a long time. Hierarchies and bureaucracies may still have their function, but they are less significant than they were to the well-being of the whole enterprise.

We have been used to a hierarchical liturgical pattern of God-Preacher/Celebrant-Musicians/Singers/Readers-Congregation. We have also been used to a hierarchical musical pattern of Composer-Conductor-Orchestra-Audience. There is room for the conductor's interpretation, possibly in consultation with the orchestra, possibly imposed upon them, and the audience, vital though it may be, participates only through listening, albeit at best with active and expectant attention. Pierre Boulez' *Répons* works differently. It needs soloists, chamber orchestra, computer, and technician, with the conductor giving cues rather than actively 'shaping' the music. The sound does not come from only one direction. All are involved in creating music (not just re-creating it) and at the same time are contributing *within* a total environment of sound. No two performances being identical, the conductor needs to be flexible as well as having such a precise understanding of the laws of sound that the flexibility is not anarchic and the performance creative. Again, authority has become diffuse and corporate.

We should stand back at this point and ask which model of authority is most congruent with that of Jesus. He was reported as speaking as one with authority. But his own comment, both in word and deed, was that great men exercise lordship over others while he was among his followers as one who serves. He regarded displays of power as an evil temptation and he refused to fulfil popular expectations of a Messiah of coercive power. He rode into Jerusalem not on a war horse but on a donkey.

If authority is most genuine when it comes from the 'author', the 'source', and so is dependable and trustworthy, then Jesus in his teaching was exercising authentic authority.

In his actions, he seems to have slowly withdrawn from dazzling displays, so bewildering and disappointing the crowds and even his closest followers that in the end all had deserted him. But he let himself be 'handed over' to the 'authorities', trusting in the authority of the vulnerable love that risks total defeat.

How can the authority of Jesus be expressed in corporate structures and relationships? Is it impracticable and naive to try? Is individual holiness the best we can hope for in the midst of an unholy world, waiting on God to lift us to heaven? In the words of the title of Reinhold Niebuhr's book, can we have 'moral man' but only an 'immoral society'? Bernice Martin wrote in the magazine *Christian* (no. 25): "Very few social systems in the history of the world have placed Love above such essential and dominant values as Order, Continuity, Power, or Hierarchy. It is deeply subversive... to place humility and worldly failure in the spiritual centre as Christianity does."[52]

Well, we might be able to discern *some* ways of at least partially fulfilling the vision of the kind of authority that Jesus exercised. To end this chapter here are a few hints to add to the suggestions about a new model of authority in a living organism.

In a play by Brecht, Galileo utters, "Happy the land that needs no heroes." We conveniently use heroes to project on them our fantasies of success or prowess or beauty. If we refused to collude with this mechanism, we would project less on to our leaders, expect less from them, not be surprised when they sometimes fail, and take more responsibility for ourselves.

Christopher Morgan, writing in a Newsletter of the Institute of Religion and Medicine in 1980 asked for "great quantities of smaller leaders of special quality."[53] He quoted the great American preacher of the nineteenth century, Phillips Brooks: "The world will get better not by the magnificent achievements of a highly gifted few, but by the patient faithfulness of the one-talented many... Heroes have done all they can, and now let common men awake and take their common tasks."[54]

We need more children to shout clearly that emperors have no clothes. We need the diffident to emerge from their shyness and make their modest contributions. We need leaders who will do their share and then be content with other and often lesser kinds of responsibility.

Phillips Brooks may make us think of personal attitudes and contributions, but we also need help in understanding how the necessities of leadership relate structurally to the whole body.

J. J. A. Vollebergh, describes 'integrated structures'.[55] By this he seeks to indicate something different from either the authoritarian or the democratic. To work well, an integrated structure needs dynamic and trusting co-operation between leader and group. Leaders have some autonomy to use their particular gifts and talents, some room for initiative and manoeuvre to use their knowledge and experience. The group co-operates with the leader, and the greater the trust the more is freedom allowed to the leader *and* the more the leader is willing to operate within the 'mandate' given by the group. (By 'mandate' he means the tasks and sphere of competence of a leader as accepted by the members of the group.) Dialogue is necessary and tension is inevitable, but these can be constructive provided a leader restrains the desire to use the organization as an instrument of personal power and the group is able to allow the leader to be more than its lackey.

Vollebergh makes the further point that there is rarely a straightforward match between person and role. The leader does not have to do everything that the leadership of a group requires. "The function of leadership then ceases to be a monolithic block and becomes a differentiated collection of roles which are distributed among people who are qualified for them."[56] Such a division of concerns can become part of the agreed mandate. Each aspect of the life of an organization has its own spokesperson. Leadership thus becomes more integrated within the organization and dialogue and confrontation are easier to admit and resolve.

Hierarchical organizations might do well to learn from the gentle and diffuse patterns of decision-making in the Society of Friends. A clerk is needed to keep track of what is happening: an authority of competence is recognized. But there is no handling down of decisions from on high. The Spirit is trusted to guide and is helped by a respectful and courteous listening one to another, a waiting in silence, and an expectation that the mind of the meeting will in time emerge and cohere.

There are parallels here with the custom in Benedictine communities. There is the same discipline of listening to one another, to those who express the past wisdom of the community, to those who are being prophetically challenging of the status quo, and to the quietest, the shyest, the least articulate. In this way the will of God is actively and prayerfully discerned. No votes are taken, no sense of a majority winning an argument. Rather does this facilitating mode of leadership keep the whole community to this listening discipline (its obedience), the abbot then expressing, and helping that community to put into effect the implications of, decisions taken when a common mind has been reached.

It is also worth paying attention to secular models of conflict resolution. Parties to a conflict are convened by a team of neutrals who neither know the outcome nor have a vested interest in any particular outcome – except in the broadest sense of a resolution satisfactory to all concerned. The task of leadership is to provide a space and atmosphere for feelings to be ventilated, stories to be told, trust to be built, and new possibilities – which had never before occurred to anybody – to emerge. The commitment of the leaders is to a future that has yet to become clear and which needs the participation of everybody present if it is to become clear.

In an imperfect world, organizations have to find ways of saying 'No' from time to time, to some who wish to become or remain members, and to some who wish to become or remain office-bearers. On occasion it may be clear to everybody that a 'No' has to be said, and the matter is handled with goodwill preserved. But it may have to be said against a person's wishes and conviction and in accordance with a concern for the common good. No organization can do without some provision, however minimal, for the use of coercive power. Otherwise there is nothing to stop the bully from forcing the way to a position of power, which power will then be exercised tyrannically. In some person or body of people there has to be invested the authority, for example, to withdraw a licence to minister, or not to recommend for a particular ministry. Care needs to be taken to find a way of saying 'No' which does what is necessary but limits the rejection and exclusion. Here are some clues.

a. The possibility of a 'No' needs to be recognized at every stage of a process of discernment that is otherwise expected to lead to a 'Yes' – to membership or office.

b. The person concerned needs to be involved in that process, to initiate his or her own profile of progress, and to work with those who have the power in such a spirit as to expect agreement to be reached. It will also help if, amongst those involved, there are one or two chosen by the person under scrutiny.

c. An appropriate appeal structure needs to be worked out in order to make power accountable and limited.

d. There is a need to recognize that some in authority find it easy to say 'No', while others find it hard. The former need to bring others into the decision-making so that they do not become persecutory, the latter so that they do not become indulgent to shortcomings, especially if temperamentally they find it hard to bear the anger of the rejected.

e. The whole process needs to be undertaken in the faith that believes that eventually an unexpected and more profound 'Yes' is latent in the 'No', a 'Yes' that can include failure in the perspective of a God who asks of us faithfulness, not success.

8

A Marked People:
Walking with God

BY way of recapitulation –

Jesus embodied to the uttermost the self-sacrificial love of God.

Jesus was often present incognito in the years before his public ministry, sometimes during it; the disciples found it hard to believe that he could be alive in something so ordinary as the breaking of bread.

Jesus engaged in public with the powers that be, as a prophet to the political and religious leaders of his day.

Jesus pioneered a new way of living and loving that left folk gasping and breathless, especially in his valuing of the despised and outcast, whose company he enjoyed, and who, he once said, would know bliss before the respectable did.

Jesus led his company of followers, enabling them to grow and learn (however obtuse they seemed), being their servant, calling them friends, and loving them to the end.

Jesus thus earned a unique authority, the most characteristic mark of which was the refusal of coercive power (no earthly throne and crown and no legions of angels to rescue him at the end), and the pursuit of vulnerable love to a crucifying death. Such was the cost and such the mark, still shown in hands and side. That it was a victorious way is a statement of faith: insofar as his disciples follow the same way, they glimpse the victory and enable others to be attracted to it.

How are those followers to be recognized? And should those who are publicly authorized and accountable be publically and immediately recognizable? Perhaps it is a 'mark' of the limitations of our loyalty that we have not received the stigmata. But few of us have even got as far as being so soaked in the Love of God that others recognize something of the presence of God in our faces. In the absence of such signs, we enter the ambiguous world of uniforms and badges.

Those who have respect for hierarchy will want to see their leaders in distinctive clothes. Otherwise they feel let down. They will wish to identify themselves through those leaders with the organization which spans centuries and continents. Their own status and destiny will be symbolized by the one who sits resplendent on a throne.

Others are repelled by copes and chasubles, whose wearers can seem haughty and pompous or awkward and ill at ease, and whose people seem unduly passive. Black gowns may be substituted, but authority is still concentrated, though now with the image of teacher and judge rather than emperor and king. The 'people' may still be passive – as it were at their desks or in the dock!

If instead of wanting to identify symbolically with the leader in special clothes, you wish to make visible a sense of corporate participation and involvement, you may appreciate a colourful chasuble as a sign of continuity and catholicity, and at the same time want to encourage everybody to look resplendent. (You might even supply tie-dyed surplices for everybody at the church door. If the cautious need a precedent, it is there in some religious communities and college chapels. And it does hide those social distinctions between suits and torn jeans.)

And there is yet more to special clothes than celebration and parties and symbolism of position and continuity. For when clothes are perceived as uniforms they communicate power. For the wearer they can boost a fragile ego or give a new recruit confidence. They can trap a person in bloated pride or add a sense of responsibility to the bearer of a corporate reputation.

Most uniforms signal a measure of coercive power delegated by a society or community. Their wearers can claim a power on behalf of others that they could never claim in their own person. Does the dog collar give a person power to act on God's behalf? Or only to some extent on behalf of the Church? And in what way? And what kind of God is implied by that action? And does such a uniform give a person a right of entry in emergencies – or just make it practically easier?

There is ambivalence here. Cassocks and Salvation Army suits may communicate responsibility, care, trustworthiness, service, but black can be forbidding and evoke fear, and for some the military analogy is disturbing.

In less hierarchical times and circumstances, those in public office may want to tone down the visual mark. A lapel cross may indicate one's faith – though one on a neck chain is probably little more than a piece of jewellery. And the symbol of the cross has become so commonplace that it is now little more than a sign. (It has of course meant terror for many a Muslim, Jew, and heretic.) But as an obvious pendant it may still be appropriate as a badge of Christian office. A ring may be a discreet indication of a deep and permanent commitment which does not impose itself on others but is not hidden away. But there is often a decorative casualness today about the wearing of rings.

The ambiguity continues. Dog collars are little more than a hundred years old. Invented in Italy, they were quickly adopted by most branches of the Church. As Anthony Russell showed they were introduced at a time of increasing specialization in society with the establishment of professional bodies, each with its unique means of identification – and often its own jargon, incomprehensible to the outsider.[57]

I wonder, Are dog collars really about control? I mean, Who holds the leash? Does the rational dominate everything? Is the only significant part of the anatomy above the neck, in the head which is split off from the rest of the body? (And if 'men' wear 'dog' collars, what do you call them when 'women' wear them?)

Uniforms therefore cannot be adopted and worn without ambiguity in what they communicate. They may merely signal a conforming to the spirit of the age. Dog collars are immediately recognizable and understood but can distance and separate a person from those around. They may be appropriate if you believe that by ordination 'clergy' enter a new order of being distinct from that of the 'laity', less so if you believe that they are simply servants of communion for the time being. After all, there is a human and institutional tendency for status to replace service as a motive. And religious communities began by simply wearing the common unremarkable clothes of the time. English clergy in the eighteenth century wore the clothes of a gentleman, the only distinctive mark being that of a white cravat. Recognizable but not intrusive? Its descendant, the white tie, is worn by some clergy today, and is probably seen by most as an expression of odd taste rather than as an item of uniform.

Such byways can be fascinating or boring according to inclination. Just a few more reflections. Do cassocks indicate a neutered sexuality, the so-called 'third' sex? What do they say about the significance or otherwise of an obviously lived or suppressed sexuality in Christian life? It is interesting to observe that women in cassocks and dog collars so wear them as not to hide their individuality or sexuality beneath a 'uniform' uniform. They find ways of integrating their clothes of office with their individual style, sometimes so subtly as to make the observer wonder a few hours later whether they were indeed wearing a uniform at all. So why bother anyway? Is there an unnecessary collusion with male hierarchical ways that women anyway are now undermining? And there is always the danger that a uniform becomes anachronistic and obsolete, surviving only in museums and quaint ceremonies of a private club.

Academic hoods are a last case in point. They originated in church at the time of the Reformation as a sign to people that the clergy were educated men and not ignorant 'mass priests'. But given the structure of training and appointments today, the sign is redundant. It may be appropriate in an educational setting but hardly elsewhere. And it does seem ludicrous that there should even be a literate's hood given to anyone authorized to conduct worship who has neither university nor theological college qualification, and that robed musicians and singers should feel the need to proclaim their academic status when everybody can tell by their performance whether they have the necessary authority to be in that position.

These matters raise passions. Arguments can be heated. So here is a list of uniforms, badges, and special clothes. What associations do they have for you? When are they appropriately worn? Are any of them redundant?

> Dog collar
> Surplice
> Cassock – black, grey, blue,
>   red, maroon, purple...
> Alb
> Scarf – black, blue
> Hood
> Stole
> Chasuble
> Gown
> White tie/cravat
> Ring
> Lapel badge
> Pendant

In asking the question, What is the unique mark of the 'priest' or 'ordained minister', it is very hard to come up with an answer. It is possible to list necessary qualities that are typical of the good Christian leader, but none of them is exclusive to the leader. In today's world such qualities as resilience, faithfulness and humour may be thought to be particularly helpful, but again they cannot be thought of as unique to the leader. In 1965 Karl Rahner spoke about the future of the church:

> "We are all one in Christ, the ultimate difference is the degree of love, for God and the brothers; distinctions of office are necessary but entirely secondary and provisional, a burden, a service, a sacred responsibility... The bishop will not look very different from any other official in a small voluntary group effectively dependent on the goodwill of that group... It will be clear and plain to see, that all dignity and

office in the church is uncovenanted service, carrying with it no honour in the world's eyes ... perhaps it will no longer constitute a profession in the social and secular sense at all."[58]

In a profound sense all the baptised are marked people – signed at Baptism on the forehead with the sign of the Cross. And this sign is a gift, and the gift is of the only status that matters – beloved of God, followers of Jesus, members of God's household. Among friends, the friends of God, it is the only mark that has meaning. Other indicators may or may not be helpful for the time being, even necessary for good order and as a reminder of responsibilities. But let us beware of the subtleties of pride.

The mark of the Cross is indelible for it signifies the profoundest truths of God. To be so marked is to enter into the inheritance of those truths, to be awed and humbled and loved. The mark is as indelible as the branded number on a beast or human arm. It is a special seal. It is our most valuable birthmark (and birthright) that cannot be erased. It reveals by second birth what the first is really all about.

No other indelible mark is needed. The mark of the Cross already implies the mark of an apostle, of the witness to the Resurrection, of the calling to be pioneers of humanity's exploration into God. And if we are all to be in some measure pioneers, then, as we saw in chapter 4, the mark will affect us deeply, throughout the organism, and its 'character' may become etched in our faces as the years go by. That 'character' will have the common 'characteristic' of a wounding struggle with all that pulls us away from true love, the struggle of the Jacob in all of us that wrestles with the mysterious stranger in the dark, and for ever after limps, though richly blessed as well. And it is for the marks of that struggle that people will look in the very being of the person to whom they then *give* authority gladly and without reserve.

"That's what the congregation want to hear – how the preacher got the scars through handling the fire of God to cauterize the wounds of the world."[59]

"(The minister) must know something of the depth of the agony and the infinite burden of the cosmic wounds of Christ by which we are healed."[60]

"We have to feed our life where all the tragedy of life is gathered to an infinite and victorious sacrifice in Christ. We are not the fire but we live where it burns."[61]

9
A Searching People:
Living with tensions

TITLES and labels can be of course be useful. It would be impossible to communicate without them. But questions need to be put to each of them:

>Does it simply describe?
>Does it too rigidly define?
>Are some more highly regarded than others?
>Do some have more weight from history?
>Are some interpreted differently among different
>   groups of people?

'Deacon' may mean 'chief layman' or 'apprentice vicar' or 'member of a lifelong order of ministry'. The word may refer to an office, to a permanent character, or to a quality of service. It is hard to see what theological justification it has as an order of the ministry of leadership, since it has been used either as a way of delegating humdrum jobs that the 'superior' clergy do not want to be bothered with or a way of finding a role for women (Anglican) or married men (Roman Catholic) without opening to them real responsibilities of leadership. A Church of England report in the seventies recommended the abolition of the diaconate. It was quietly forgotten, I suspect because the pressures of custom and the power of the tradition of the three ministries of 'bishop', 'priest' and 'deacon' was too strong.

Indeed we now find reports throughout the churches arguing for the value of a 'permanent diaconate'. They do not seem to me to take seriously enough the fact that this 'order' of ministry has never in the history of the Church found a consistent and continuing place. And it is interesting to note that a more recent report for the Church of England suggests that a deacon's areas of service might well be in health, education, and social work

99

Now these are precisely those concerns of public life where we seem to be most comfortable with women. And the question has to be pressed, What makes the service of deacons in such places ministerial in any sense other than the ones described in the chapters of this book? Of course the contribution of Christian people in secular life needs to be characterized by the spirit of service and they need to be recognized by the Church for particular 'service' and 'function' if they are to take on a representative role. But is anything else really needed?

Moreover, if a specific liturgical role is carved out for deacons at the Eucharist, emphasizing the servant nature of ministry (one could see this visually if they 'lay the table', but not so easily if they read the Gospel), does not this isolate the presiding minister even more in a position of power and as a separate caste, and does it not take away from members of the congregation tasks that they can do just as well, such as reading and preparing the table and helping to distribute communion? (It will be argued later in this chapter that the role of 'president' needs to be and look more like that of waiter than it usually does if the worship of the people is to be most effectively served.)

If all publicly recognized and accountable ministries were truly characterized by 'diakonia', we would be less bothered to create categories and 'orders'. 'Diakonia' is an essential dimension of all ministry, not exclusively distinctive. It is indeed permanent but not as an order of being. Everyone in public ministry, even a universal pastor, is to be seen as 'a servant of the servants of God', to live as 'a suffering servant'. 'Orders' become corrupted by an unnecessary overemphasis on status and hierarchy. They encourage all manner of projections and expectations, thus straitjacketing the community and overburdening the leaders. Better the verbs of process than the nouns of status: the first enables relationships, the second so easily leads to isolation and exclusion. Rather than extract a person from the people to an elevated position of power, which leads logically to the position that only the hierarchy is essential to the continuing life of the Church, let us describe accurately and modestly the new roles and relationships which are opened up to those who are entering a particular public ministry.

By toning down such ministries and making them 'for the time being' rather than 'for the rest of time', ministers themselves will not be tempted to bury their uniqueness in God under the weight of their role or to lose touch with the secular world. There is no need for human beings to have only one mode of relationship to the community for life. The 'permanence' is again in the serving-sacrificial quality of life and not in any particular form of ministry.

'Priest' and 'Minister' carry different weight and different associations according to denomination – 'priest' sounds more Catholic, 'minister' more Protestant. The first can sometimes carry the association of 'the real thing', the second as 'only half-way there'. Or 'priest' may be regarded as one who uses 'priestcraft' to maintain a powerful intermediary position between human beings and God.

Might it help if we confined the use of the word 'priest' to refer to

> *a.* the sacrificial character of Christian life, i.e. 'priestly';
> *b.* the calling of all Christian people to be a 'royal priesthood';
> *c.* the priesthood of Christ as a metaphor of expended love.

Again, 'minister' may best be used as a verb to indicate the servant character of Christian life.

'Presbyter' seems to be the most appropriate title for the leader of the Christian community (it was adopted instead of 'priest' by the Church of South India). And might it not be appropriate whatever the geographical area of responsibility? There would be the presbyter of a parish and the presbyter of a Diocese or Province of wherever. The newly trained and commissioned and those serving part-time in a parish would be 'assistant presbyters'. And all of them are the 'servants of communion'.

Where ministry to institutions and networks is concerned, 'chaplain' seems an uncontentious title, parallel to 'presbyter'.

Others who minister publicly in the Church's name could be commissioned as and known simply by the ministry itself –

Missionary, Evangelist, Teacher, Preacher, Healer, Coun-
sellor, Administrator, Musician, Verger.

It hardly needs adding that old titles will disappear slowly if at all,
even if these suggestions can, I contend, be respectably argued
and even if catholicity and continuity on the one hand and the
integrity of the local church on the other could be shown not to
have been compromised. But the exercise of asking if we can do
without the titles of bishop, priest, deacon, minister, is to
encourage us to think through our own responses to what we
have inherited. We do well to be articulate about our differences
and live with them, bearing any lack of resolution and not
making decisions that increase our own and others' burdens.

It might be helpful at this point to recall that there are certain
biblical principles about ministry that can be discerned in the
pages of the Scriptures, reflecting the experience of the first
Christians. They remind us of the tensions between institution
and organism, formality and informality, spontaneous gift and
continuing office, tensions that are always present and may in
fact be needed to prevent any one of us claiming total truth and
to encourage the appreciation of different approaches for the
sake of the well-being of the whole.

- *a.* God calls and enables people to minister.
- *b.* The call is to meet a specific need.
- *c.* Ministries are varied, shared, complementary.
- *d.* Ministries are not necessarily linked to specific functions in
  worship, though some will be.
- *e.* There are ministries which involve travel, especially those
  of oversight and training.
- *f.* There are ministries which are tied to one place.
- *g.* There are ministries which are primarily concerned to
  equip members.
- *h.* There are ministries which are primarily concerned with
  the world around.
- *i.* There is no exclusive giving or receiving – always
  mutuality.

St Paul laid foundations and moved on, and indicated that among the new communities there were people with many gifts for building up the Body, among them that of leadership, but with no special name or status. To the Thessalonians he wrote, "Respect those who labour among you, lead you in the Lord, and admonish you."[62]

If the status of public ministries is toned down, we create space for the true significance of Baptism to emerge. It becomes THE important occasion of a beginning, and, like subsequent expressions of it, has the elements of recognition, affirmation, dedication, and blessing. Focused in a single moment is that mark of Christian character which becomes indelible over the years as the significance of the Baptism is lived ever more deeply.

Confirmation then becomes the affirmation of adult responsibility for ministry in the name of Christ and the Church, and also includes dedication, and blessing – the empowerment of the Holy Spirit, again the 'seal', the indelible 'mark'. George Bell as Bishop of Chichester used to interpolate in the service of Confirmation the words, "Take thou authority to exercise the ministry of a lay person in the Church of God." And from Confirmation flow all the ministries, both hidden within and engaged with society.

It is in Baptism/Confirmation that we show forth our *humanity* in Christ. We use water, the universal life-giver; we use oil, symbol of the consecration of the whole of life to God; we use hands with prayer to signify empowerment for discipleship, for following the Way. The emphasis is not so much on the *moment* of physical birth or of personal rebirth as on a new beginning moment for the person-in-community and for the community as a whole who recognize that a new human being is being brought into their midst, 'incorporated', joined to the Body. It is a moment of co-inherence, of the living organism demonstrating that *this* person, *this* local church, and the worldwide communion of churches are organically related to one another in Christ. And by this act all the relationships in the community shift a little: nothing is ever quite the same again.

The commissioning of a public minister is another beginning

moment which draws out further some of the implications of Baptism. It gives a person a particular place and relationship in the community's 'order' of being and doing, a new relationship of accountable service, a new function ('ordo') in the Body. Again the relationship is organic. The minister is not inserted from 'above' but moves into a different relationship to the whole from that which existed before that moment. (In another sense of course all is indeed 'from above', from the free transcendent God, but the God we believe is Beyond waits to be discovered within and among us, as incarnate in us and committed to us, and consequently beholden to our response.)

Such beginning moments are necessary from time to time, commissioning to particular ministries, from the small-scale, local to one place or association, temporary, non-transferable, unpaid, after modest preparation, to the larger scale, with greater responsibilities, in principle for many years, transferable, paid, after considerable training. A modest place in this structure is still allowed to archbishops and even popes – perhaps by more modest names!

Seriously though, if we continue to put at the *centre* of our thinking about ministry those vicars and bishops who are full-time and stipendiary, then all reports about possible reforms and diversification will end up as appeals for prayer for more priests, together with reluctant publicity. If we put Baptism/Confirmation at the centre of our thinking, there could be a new flowering of ministries, with everybody released for contributions that really are and also look like those of servants and friends.

Of course there are many other issues here, not least in our day around sexuality and gender. It is a rueful reflection that the pressure on the ministry of leadership and its shortages would be considerably relieved if, in varying measure in the different churches, women, gay men, and married men could in principle be *welcomed* as potential vicars and bishops, rather than so often excluded. I wonder if our reluctance to do this hints at the disturbance all such people can sometimes cause because they are inevitably perceived as sexually active beings. The high status of the celibate priest is called into question along with the centrality of male hierarchical power. And if 'clergy' in lifestyle are no different from 'laity' then where is their distinctiveness? If clergy are sexually active, then where is the 'sign' pointing to heaven and the eternal? But therein lies the precise point. If we truly believe in the doctrines of Creation and Incarnation, there can be no distinctions in spirituality and holiness: they must be expressed from the within of the human, the sexual, the earthed. To pretend otherwise is to court the danger of the supposedly asexual, 'spiritual', ecclesiastical functionary who cannot relax with ordinary humanity and whose voice shows that he has lost touch with his own deeper self and with God.

We are now realizing that the participation of women in the ministry of leadership is raising other profound questions about the character of that ministry – questions which take us beyond the issue of whether or not women can be presbyters. Kathleen Bliss saw this as long ago now as 1952.[63] For many of us it is only recently that we have begun to feel the pressure of these questions. We might well have come to the point of agreeing that all public offices in the Church should be open to women in the same way as they are open to men. But we may find it vaguely disturbing and confusing that because women have begun to share more power in the life of the Church we are all being challenged – men and women alike – to search for new patterns of leadership.

A particular memory of my lack of awareness is still vivid. I was a curate at the parish church in Stretford near Manchester in the late sixties where the chief (and that word felt appropriate) flower arranger knew that she was the only woman to enter the sanctuary – reverently to put stand and vases in their place. "A privilege, Rector," she used to say. I remember feeling uneasy but there was not the context of disturbance and discussion to pursue that unease beyond the thought that she was strictly speaking inaccurate – a cleaner, also of course a woman, went into the sanctuary too. We were indeed all trapped.

Going back to my childhood, I recall the adults around me

being impressed by the preaching of a woman in the Methodist Church we went to. Very rarely did we see one in the pulpit. Fortunate for her that she was good. For even today if a woman should preach badly, the prejudiced would say that it simply shows that women are bad at preaching, while the discerning would either want to help her do better or encourage her to engage in another kind of ministry. But if a man should preach badly, the first thoughts might be that he was having an off-day or, if the performance were typical, that we would just have to put up with it for the sake of the other gifts he undoubtedly had.

More recently, what women have been saying and demonstrating for decades has reached beyond the confines of the smaller churches and is now challenging the ways of hierarchy and patriarchy. As a single example of much that has been happening, I would mention the service that Lavinia Byrne has done in making available a selection of women's writings about faith and ministry.[64] I was surprised – though I shouldn't have been – to see just how much of the history of the contribution of women in the life of the Church hardly ever gets mentioned.

For example, of women in the Salvation Army during the First World War, Evangeline Booth wrote in 1930 that there was nothing of disease and degradation that they had not faced with 'steady eyes'.[65] Isabella Gilmore, who pioneered women's ministry in the Church of England, knew that women more than men have learned 'to help without doing harm.'[66] They could both rightly challenge men to look in a similar unflinching way on their own and others' hurts. (Less able and willing to do so, they might be thought to be thereby *less* qualified for public ministry.)

In an address in 1909 Catherine Booth pointed out that it was a woman who had been commissioned by the risen Christ to tell the apostles of his resurrection:

> "Not she with traitorous lips her Saviour stung,
> Not she denied him with unholy tongue;
> She, whilst apostles shrunk, could danger brave;
> Last at the cross, and earliest at the grave."[67]

It is the dates of such contributions that fascinate us now. In 1911 Hatty Baker wrote: "There must be behind the universe, in and through the universe, a heart like a woman's, tender, pitiful, compassionate, faithful, loving to the end, to death, and we need – we surely need a woman as well as a man to interpret the heart of our Mother-Father God."[68] And there are still those who claim it is heretical to address God as Mother...

Again, Maude Royden wrote in 1924: "If the words of Christ were isolated from their context and read to one to whom the gospels were not familiar it would be absolutely impossible for him to guess whether any special word or phrase was addressed to a woman or to a man."[69]

Those are merely samples, mentioned not to trivialize an important issue, but to enable us to recognize that human beings make choices about what they write, publish, read, and recommend. We may think we are learning of what is most significant, but what comes our way is filtered by those who have the power over what is made available.

Now it is clear from the quotations that Lavinia Byrne has garnered that women *have already* ministered publicly in all the ways indicated in this book. But because there have not been enough women, for long enough, both to be *commissioned* for that ministry and also to exert such influence as to change the structure of the patterns of ministry, too many of them have been easily forgotten.

Just as women are beginning to be given responsibility in the ministry of leadership it might seem tactless and even cruel to cast doubt on the particular structure we have inherited. But I believe it is the more obvious presence of women in such positions that is pressing the question for all those in public office: Which is more important to me, my being 'ordained' or my being baptized? If the former, what does that do to my sense of priorities – and what does it do to those who are not 'ordained'?

Clifford Longley writing in *The Times* in February 1981 commented on the argument being put forward in Roman Catholic circles that it is Baptism that is the basis for Christian unity across present divides: "Groups of baptized Christians organized in structured communities can recognize themselves and each other as churches faithful to the apostolic tradition, by recognizing a common apostolic faith."[70]

If that is the perspective, that such churches are already united, it makes questions about the ministry of leadership less significant or crucial. We may also begin to relax, and come to understand that women and men *together* have so much to offer if they can stop their mutual suspicion and isolation. *Together* they may discover something new from God.

Vincent Donovan has argued the need to simplify our understanding and practice of 'ordination'.[71] From his experience of leadership emerging in the midst of the community, he saw that all that was needed was for the bishop, representing in his person the wider church, to visit the local church to recognize a new leader as the accepted sign of the presence of the Christ who had come in faith and baptism to them all, and that consequently they were a true part of the universal church, a real eucharistic community. The 'ordination' was not so much that of the individual as of the whole community, a consecration of *all* the offices and gifts and functions of the body.

The commissioning of such a new presbyter needs a complementary emphasis on the re-dedication and blessing of the whole people. Indeed if the latter is lived and seen as primary, and if in worship this has been enacted, then the new presbyter is brought into the proceedings quite modestly near the end, perhaps with some such words as these:

> "And finally we greet you, N, welcoming and naming you as the one among us called and fit to be our presbyter. You have heard and seen how many and varied are the gifts exercised among us for the common good, for the worship and mission of God. As a people we have been entrusted in baptism with the power and responsibility to be the church in this place, a eucharistic community in mission, and we recognize you as the one called by God to lead us. We ask the presbyter of our diocese, N our bishop, on behalf of the wider communion of churches to which we belong, to receive your dedication, to commission you in our and Christ's name, and with us to bless you

with prayer and the laying on of hands, thanking God for all the blessings we receive and asking the Holy Spirit to empower us in Christ's service."

Would anything crucial be lost then, if there were no 'orders' of ministry as such, only various more modest forms of beginnings by means of 'commissioning'? Behind the notion of 'orders' is an understanding of life and the 'ordering' of creation and of corporate bodies that is static – once a priest always a priest, once a nobleman always a nobleman (in his castle), once a peasant always a peasant (at his gate), once a monarch always a monarch. Talk of being 'elevated' or 'translated' into a new order of being no longer makes sense if organizations are more like organisms, ordered and harmonious but fluid and flexible in ongoing life – not least in a complex and fast-changing world. And while this sits more easily with a great variety of ministries, it is not to deny the need for leadership nor the value in the past of a hierarchical ordering. But it is to say that a more static order may be one of the worst responses now to the need for an ordered harmony. Too many people no longer fit and increasingly get hurt.

Faced with acronyms like MOW (Movement for the Ordination of Women), WAOW (Women Against the Ordination of Women), and MOMM (Movement for the Ordination of Married Men), the subversive and impish part of me wants to inaugurate MUM (Movement for the Unfrocking of Men)...

❖

Nicholas Harvey has written, "What is threatened by the suggestion that the only reason we continue to have ordained priesthood is that we haven't yet managed to live without it? Only, I suggest, our entrenched but unconscious paganism, which prompts us to have priests to control the sacred, and to take responsibility for our sins, thus enabling us to remain children a little longer."[72]

❖

Again, this is not to deny the need for a demanding and different pattern of leadership in the churches from that which is found where the few lord it over the many. If we had more modest beginnings of ministries that were expected to last only a few years before a person would move to something else, then we see the value of a kind of 'curriculum vitae' of ministry, or a profile of past ministries which would be pertinent in assessing a person's suitability for a particular appointment. It is not hard to think of some relevant questions:

> What is the quality of the person's loving – in friendship, intimate relationships, service, sacrifice, wisdom?
>
> How has the person already been ministering, incognito and engaged with the secular world?
>
> What is the person's experience and understanding of apostolic, pioneering ministry?
>
> On what scale, with what degree of responsibility, has this person experienced and understood the ministry of leadership, servant of communion?

Where those questions can be answered positively, and experience and understanding has grown, a person's worth and suitability for 'high' office can be discerned. But even then, the 'presbyter' concerned, even if called 'presiding presbyter commonly called bishop', will be appointed for the time being as the person most truly able to enable, embody, and represent the People of God in Christ.

It may well be that we should expect our leaders to retire or resign at an earlier age than is customary. Do some continue because of this notion of 'once a priest always a priest'? Clearly a community would be foolish to lose the benefit of its wise guides, those for whom that wisdom and guidance are indelibly part of their lives and character.

Yes, in a sense such a person never retires. Like a wood carver or a composer you may never 'retire' from that which gives your life purpose and direction and fulfilment. If your characteristic place is on the threshold, conducting rites of passage, if you really come alive with pencil and paper to hand, you won't give these up just because you have reached a pensionable age. You will go on working until you are incapable – even if you may need honest friends to tell you when. And of course the Christian vocation to service-sacrifice-friendship is never done. But for the good of the whole community it may be wise if those who lead do not hang on to office – even that of pope or monarch. If we have found ways of valuing the services of retired archbishops and queen mothers when they no longer occupy their 'chair', we should not find it impossible to value and use former presbyters in all kinds of ministry. There is also of course a curious freedom and delight in being relieved of the burdens of representative office. As long as you have enough to live on, you do not have to be paid directly for what you do and you do not have to be so guarded about what you say. Let the elderly dream dreams and become prophets that disturb!

The location of a sense of *being* is not in people's ministry but in their *humanity,* and in the expression and focus of the deepest truths of that humanity in being baptized. Each one of us is eternally delighted in, just as we are. We do not have to earn our worth. We are valued by Love for ever. And the blessings and promises of Baptism are all-embracing enough to allow within their working out all manner of changes in lesser commitments.

Also this; 'Being' is not to be understood as a static *thing*. Each of us is in flux, dynamic, growing, our deeds contributing to the kind of person we are in the process of becoming. Of course we need structures – like the skeleton – but we are more than the skeleton, bound for a destiny more glorious than a skull in a grave.

So roles need not be so fixed and separating that we cannot be human by means of them, nor so ill-defined that without any framework we are rendered ineffective.

All labels are in the end to be done away with, especially when they become a defence against being known for who we are. The only reason for a Christian to enter public ministry is, in the end, odd as it may seem, simply that it is the best, and perhaps the only way, that God can draw that person more deeply into the ways of friendship and love. That is what it is all about, power serving love among the friends of God.

Given that the argument in this chapter has been for a more modest approach to the ministry of leadership than in patriarchal and hierarchical days, what might this imply for the role of the presbyter at the Eucharist? How central need it be? If it be said that the presbyter 'represents' Christ by presiding at this central act of Christian worship, does he or she so represent in a way that is different from that of anybody else present, whether visibly taking part in the leading of the worship or not? Here if anywhere the whole Christian community is surely aiming to make its Christlikeness most typically visible. So the leader must take care not to demonstrate a pattern of leadership that is alien to the Spirit of Christ.

Taking an analogy from the theatre, it might then be argued that the role of the leader is more like that of producer of the drama than that of leading actor. We might describe the necessary role of such a person as that of being responsible for making sure that it is a Christian Eucharist that is celebrated when a particular congregation gathers for worship.

(We may actually be familiar with one instance of the leader of worship as 'producer', exercising an 'episcopal' role of guarding and focusing. Sometimes bishops are present and visible throughout an act of worship and are seen and heard to do nothing but articulate God's blessing at the end. Looked at in one way they are having an evening off, but their presence assures us that the proceedings are within the Christian 'frame' and the modest contribution is perhaps appropriate to the serving-sacrificial model of leadership that is embedded in the whole of the diaconal-priestly community.)

Taking an analogy from a meal in a restaurant, the leading role might be akin to that of the waiter, whose success is measured by the degree to which he or she is least noticed. The role of the servant is to decrease in order that the one being served may increase. It is to enable the living presence of the Other and of the others, that the people present may more really and truly meet with the Risen Christ. The clue that reveals how far most celebrations have strayed is the practice of those presiding receiving communion first. What waiter – or host – would do that? The guests are there to be served first. The story is told of a cathedral Eucharist where the supply of consecrated bread and wine ran out completely with a dozen or so people not having received. A shrewd verger commented to the clergy afterwards, "There'd have been enough to go round if you lot hadn't helped yourselves first." So the question is put, How best can the presbyter be the 'servant of communion' at the Eucharist?

John Fenton has wryly pointed out[73] that there has been more talk in the Christian 'restaurant' about the waiters and waitresses than about the meal. There have been more disputes about ministry than about the Gospel. Yet waiters at their best are unobtrusive, supplying what is necessary and otherwise keeping in the background. Even hosts do not intrude: they welcome, introduce guests to one another, mention someone or something special, and bid farewell. They watch over the proceedings, holding the occasion together, but the party is celebrated by all. The host must remember what it is like to be a waiter, must indeed 'lead' only in that kind of spirit. Otherwise he or she will be tempted to take advantage of the vulnerability of the guests, dominating and manipulating them. Hosts are still servants – indeed slaves, not in the sense of having no freedom (though they are indeed beholden to their guests) but in having nothing to do with systems of rank.

That is not all. If we are to make sure that it is *Christ* who is clearly represented by a human being at the Eucharist, is it *really* obvious (as seems by custom) that it should always be the leader of the community in the limelight, wearing hieratic clothes, standing in a special place apart, making the significant actions and saying the significant words, and being male?

If Christ is most truly to be seen to be 'present' in those outside the gates of respectability and acceptability, should not the one who, at the very least, breaks the bread be, in turn, the orphaned child, the camp queen, the mentally handicapped, the black lesbian? If Paul's ministry was fulfilled despite his handicap (his 'thorn in the flesh'), perhaps even because of it, we might take comfort and *expect* those in positions of *Christian* leadership to be burdened in some significant way, have something in their lives which is problematic and prone to disaster – either because of some persistent weakness of their own or by what others impose on them.[74] We need to ask who in our communities can be the most vivid and efficacious 'sign' of the vulnerable and the outcast, and so most aptly show forth Christ.

Such 'outsiders' always call the community into a more generous and inclusive way of living. They disturb the complacent. So the leader cannot simply focus a unity that already is in existence. There is too much hostility, too much suspicion of those who are strange and different, too many disagreements. The focus has also to be on the future. Those in positions of leadership need to bear within themselves the tensions of what is unresolved, seeking ways to work with and through the conflicts. In any case truth is rich and complex and full of paradoxes. So should not the leader represent, not a conforming unison but *God's* longing for harmony?[75]

This is no recipe for chaos. At the Eucharist of course we need table-preparers, bread-breakers, communion servers and somebody who knows who does what when and where, and has enabled them to do it prayerfully and without fuss. And of course this kind of preparation is more demanding of the leader than the autocratic style of the leading actor – whether in Catholic or Protestant versions. Where few people are gathered, little needs preparation; where there are hundreds inevitably more time and skill are needed: the contrast is similar over catering arrangements!

Here is a possible ground plan for a small company, hinting at the cellular structure of the organism: the circle is open, a cross is suspended over a window, Both cross and window give some sense of the beyond, and the circle is not closed in on itself.

Here is a possible ground plan for a larger company of up to sixty people.

On this scale, the openness to the beyond can be represented by a cross suspended above the central table. The arrows indicate the places of four ministrants who prepare the central table, having received a roll of bread, a plate, a jug of wine, and an empty goblet from each cell. They may also conveniently break the bread, pour the wine into goblets, and either administer communion around the cell nearest to them (as indicated by the arrows) or pass bread and wine to their neighbour, who, having received, passes them on until they reach the next ministrant.

The number of cells can of course be multiplied in each direction for larger gatherings, and each cell can accommodate an extra chair or two without difficulty. But the image is of the living cell and the larger organism, interdependent, the one complete in itself, the other made up of the cells but as a whole expressing a greater reality than each of the cells in itself. And the presbyter can take a back seat during the celebration and perhaps introduce the prayers by bringing together the concerns of the community in the notices for the week...

✤

NB 1

A parallel question is this. How can the presbyter best enable Christian people to be ministers of reconciliation to one another? If the loosening power of forgiveness has been given to the whole Church and not just to the presbyters, then we have another instance of how a modest role has been distorted into the building up of exclusive power and the spreading of fear rather than of love.

NB 2

Congenial to this approach is the increasing practice of books for worship providing an outline of the structure of services and a quarry of alternative material rather than one unalterable set of words. There is still a sense of boundary keeping, that within certain parameters there can be a variety of patterns of worship, and that outside them patterns will at best be experimental and sometimes less than fully Christian.

A People who Pray and Risk:
Acting as if

To reflect prayerfully then on the human meaning of Christian ministries:

Love as service and care—the towel:

> We are to take courage and serve others, especially the very old and the very young, and those we shy away from, in humdrum, often hidden deeds of kindness. "Wash one another's feet."

> We are to take the towel and through a caring touch make others feel warmed and accepted, whoever they are and however low and rejected they feel, as we ourselves may also feel.

> The towel is a sign of the love that is service. It is a sign of the stature of our humanity, of our ministry of 'deaconing'. It is part of our human vocation to embrace it humbly and joyfully.

Love as sacrifice and pain-bearing—the cross:

> We are to take courage and put ourselves out for others, in prayer and action. This is service as it becomes costly, perhaps wearisome and calling for endurance, perhaps painful in the bearing of burdens. The more we are aware of the immovable parts of our own pain and press gently into them, the more we sense, through sight and hearing and intuition, the pain of others and of the whole creation.

We are to take the cross and through its healing touch make others feel that they are not alone, but belong to the same fellowship of pain in which we also participate.

The cross is a sign of the love that is sacrifice. It is a sign of the stature of our humanity, of our 'priestly' ministry. It is part of our human vocation to embrace it humbly and joyfully.

Love as discernment and guidance — the shepherd's crook:

We are to take courage and guide others, by word and deed, especially our friends and those who are young. Through the only authority that is authentic, that frees and does not dominate, an authority earned through service and sacrifice, so costly as to identify with the worst in others, accepting them as they are and enjoying their company, whatever damage they may do to our 'reputation', being present to them and with them in their pain. We can then go on to challenge both them and those who may have harmed them to follow the same deeply human way, of service and sacrifice, on which we stumble too. We cannot force anyone to follow, we cannot always stop people harming themselves or others, but we can warn and we can encourage.

We are to take the shepherd's crook and through its firm and gentle touch make others feel that the way in which they live does matter, and what is at present beyond us is worth discerning and striving for, and that much in the past needs healing and release.

The crook is the sign of love that is discernment. It too is a sign of the stature of our humanity, of our 'episcopal' ministry. It is part of our human vocation to embrace it humbly and joyfully.

All three symbols speak of small things, of a way that at heart demands no great skill or learning. To take it to ourselves is to live in a truly human manner. Whether in hidden or public ways, we are called to embody this love, to represent this love, to enable others to embrace this love. It is at the heart of the life of the baptized, the heart of ministry, and the heart of humanity. It is given for the maturing and flourishing of ourselves and others. Through it God is unfolded in the world.

In this perspective those among us who are called to the ministry of leadership, whether in places of work, in local communities, in organisations and institutions, or in churches, whether in pioneering or well established contexts, have the task of enabling the good of the whole, of representing the whole to others, and of embodying its values in themselves, living organisms in the greater body.

If you feel trapped, either in a ministry which does not seem to fit your vocation or unable to enter a ministry to which you feel called – and if you find that the framework that has been sketched in these pages makes sense – you have to work for structural change and in so far as it is possible (not least within yourself) you have to act and be as if the changes have already taken place. You talk and network with others of like mind, even discover others near you probably to the surprise of everyone. If you think deeply, pray longingly, and live faithfully through the dislocation that has come from the drying up of the wells or the tearing apart within or exclusion from the current order of things, then you will exert a significant influence. It is power of a kind, but not that of place or position.

To act 'as if' actually has a respectable ecclesiastical history. In the Middle Ages there was developed the theory of *non acceptatio legis* – a rejection of law from above by opposition at the base. Such temporary illegality was recognized as legitimate. So it must always be as long as large-scale societies exist. Experiments cannot claim to be characteristic of the whole: otherwise they have no point. Nor can they make their claims prematurely. And by their nature they will often conflict with what is established and customary.

For example, we may no longer receive into our hearts and minds a particular doctrine. It does not carry conviction – at least in the form in which it is presented. The 'common-sensus' of the faithful is withdrawn, often slowly, usually silently, thus creating a vacuum. At the right moment, an experiment that has proved its worth can enter the space vacated. That which does not speak to our condition, either in the resonances of truth or on the encouragement of hope or in the astringency of challenge, we simply do not receive into ourselves. So some teachings fade, such as a divine order which necessitates slavery, and new teaching takes its place. Resolutions of synods come at the end of this process. What was an experiment now becomes characteristic of the whole community.

In one way all of us are bound to behave thus. For we are called to act and be as if the Love of God really did flourish through the universe. Of course there may come a point when the tensions of public ministry become too great. You may recognize that you have suffered 'spiritual abuse' for years, as woman, as gay man, as black. So you have to resign and let your ability to minister be latent. But if you have a particular ministry in the attic, there is no need to do nothing – and so become bitter and resentful. You have to search for other ways of being fulfilled. Again, act and be *as if*, with integrity, yes, but without claiming that all is well with you and all is wrong with them. For then you would be self-righteous, forgetting that none of us is uncorrupted. Be wily, compromise if need be, even 'sin boldly', certainly find your angry and loving language and so be compassionate. And like the cartoonist, treat neither yourself nor the Church solemnly. Hear the chuckle in the belly of God...

Sources and Acknowledgments

THE author has been sustained and challenged by many conversations about ministry, both with people in the flesh and also, silently, with writers through their works. He has absorbed much of this without now being able to separate his own thinking from that of others. But he is able to trace many of the more direct debts of gratitude and a list of these appears here. In one or two instances he is unable to remember any more details than a writer's name and he apologizes if here or in any other references copyright has been infringed. Amends will be made in any future edition of this book.

1 These lines echo T. S. Eliot in his poem *Four Quartets*. And I think he may well himself have been echoing someone else in his turn!

2 A phrase used by Daniel Halévy in his life of Charles Péguy.

3 The question put in the Baptism Service in the Alternative Service Book of the Church of England, 1980.

4 A word whose meaning ranges deeper and wider than the word 'repentance' by which it is usually translated.

5 Paraphrasing part of 1 Corinthians 13.

6 1 Peter 2.5, 9

7 Hebrews 5.6, 10

8 A direct quotation from R. C. Moberley's book *Ministerial Priesthood*, published by John Murray as long ago now as 1919.

9 Expressed by Peter Hebblethwaite in his readable *In the Vatican*, published by the Oxford University Press in 1987.

10 From the experience of those living in the shadow of secret police, in Petru Dumitriu's novel about life in Communist Romania, *Incognito*, published in England by Collins in 1964.

11 Job 23.8–9

12 I have not been able to trace this typical remark of Simone Weil.

13 Revelation 2.17

14 Dorothy Sayers arguing against churchianity in her book *Creed or Chaos,* published by Harcourt Brace in 1949.

15 From papers produced by the Laity Project at Andover Newton Theological School in Massachusetts, 1981.

16 Margaret Kane has written of her ministry of making connections between Christianity and the world of industry. This question comes from her book *Theology in an Industrial Society,* published by SCM Press in 1975.

17 Pope Pius XII.

18 A classic conviction of Dietrich Bonhoeffer in his *Letters and Papers from Prison,* published in England by the SCM Press, 1953 and 1967.

19 See 15.

20 See 15.

21 A typically judicious statement by Geoffrey Lampe in one of his essays collected in *Explorations in Theology 8* and published by the SCM Press in 1981.

22 From Vincent Donovan's thought-provoking account of his missionary work among the Masai of East Africa, *Christianity Rediscovered,* published originally in America and by the SCM Press in London in 1982.

23 The passionate conviction of Frances Young and Kenneth Wilson in their jointly written book *Focus on God,* published by the Epworth Press in 1986.

24 Lucas Grollenberg edited a collection of Dutch essays on ministry called *Minister? Pastor? Prophet?* which was published in English by the SCM Press in 1980. An important chapter from which this challenge comes is by J. J. A. Vollebergh and entitled *Religious Leadership.*

25 John Drury makes reference to these three figures in one of his books. I apologize that I have been unable to trace the reference.

26 From an influential report of the world Council of Churches, *Baptism, Eucharist, and Ministry,* which has provoked much reflection among the member churches during the eighties.

27 From one of Edward Schillebeeckx' books critical of much current Roman Catholic practice, *Ministry,* published in English by the SCM Press in 1980.

28 From the *Newsletter of Ministers at Work* no. 2.

29 See 28.

30 From a student on a course directed by the author for the Ministerial Training Scheme in the Diocese of St Albans from 1982–85.

31 Michael Ranken has done much to help forward our thinking about ministry in the midst of the secular and this quotation comes from an article he wrote for the magazine *Theology* in March 1982, and is used with permission.

32 See 31.

33 See 31.

34 Ezekiel 3.15

35 Proverbs 31.8–9

36 I have cherished this quotation from Pierre Teilhard de Chardin for so many years that I have mislaid its source.

37 Loren Eiseley wrote within the great tradition of American observers and interpreters of the natural world. These quotations come from the title essay of a collection called *The Star Thrower*, published by Wildwood in 1978. Permission sought.

38 See 37.

39 See 37.

40 See 37.

41 Hans Küng's re-evaluation of the theology of ministry can be found in his book, *Why Priests?*, published by Fontana in 1972.

42 See 26.

43 These distinctions are helpfully described in Kenneth Mason's book, *Priesthood and Society*, published by the Canterbury Press in 1992.

44 See 26.

45 See 27.

46 A selection of Roland Allen's work was reprinted by Eerdmans in 1983, edited by David Paton and Charles Long under the title of *The Compulsion of the Spirit*. Roland Allen was writing prophetically at the beginning of the century.

47 See 22.

48 Anthony Russell provided a thorough survey with fascinating detail of the way in which the clergy became a profession over the last two centuries. His book is called *The Clerical Profession* and was published by SPCK in 1980.

49 I believe I came across this remark by David Stafford-Clark in another author's book, but I am afraid I have lost the reference.

50 See 22.

51 Fritzjof Capra is one of those who has discerned that humanity is in the midst of a profound paradigm shift in science, philosophy, and religion. He writes of these things in an accessible way in *The Turning Point,* published by Wildwood in 1982.

52 From an article by Bernice Martin in the magazine *Christian,* no. 25, 1982.

53 From an article by Christopher Morgan in the Newsletter of the Institute of Religion and Medicine in 1980.

54 Phillips Brooks is quoted in Christopher Morgan's article – see 55.

55 See 24.

56 See 24.

57 See 48.

58 The much respected German Roman Catholic theologian Karl Rahner is quoted by Terence Card in his book *Priesthood and Ministry in Crisis* published by SCM in 1988.

59 From a book on preaching by the Methodist Colin Morris entitled *The Word and the Words* and published by the Epworth Press in 1975.

60 Ruth Matthews used this quotation from Daniel Jenkins in an essay called *On Ordination and Ministry* in a collection entitled *The Experience of Ordination,* edited by Kenneth Wilson and published by Epworth in 1979.

61 Within the quotation by Daniel Jenkins in the previous reference is this sentence by the great Congregational preacher and theologian, P. T. Forsyth.

62 1 Thessalonians 5.12.

63 Kathleen Bliss wrote of these things in *The Service of Women in the Church,* published by the SCM Press in 1952.

64 I owe the next five references to Lavinia Byrne's collection of quotations from women's spiritual writings called *The Hidden Tradition* and published by SPCK in 1991.

65 Evangeline Booth in *Woman*, published by Fleming H. Russell in New York in 1930.

66 Janet Grierson quotes this phrase of Isabella Gilmore in her biography of that name published by SPCK in 1962.

67 Catherine Booth giving an address on *Female Ministry* in 1909.

68 Hatty Baker wrote *Women in the Ministry* in 1911.

69 Maude Royden wrote *The Church and Women* in 1924.

70 Clifford Longley is the Religious Affairs Correspondent for *The Times*. This is from an article that appeared in February 1981.

71 See 22.

72 Nicholas Harvey wrote an article called *Women's Ordination: a sideways look* in *The Month*, June 1991.

73 John Fenton regularly writes a short commentary on the Sunday readings in the Church of England's lectionary in the *Church Times*. These remarks come from his article in the issue dated 21 February 1992.

74 See 73.

75 Peter Selby addressed this theme in his book *Belonging,* published by SPCK in 1991.